I LOVE HER,

THAT'S WHY!

AN AUTOBIOGRAPHY

BY

George Burns

WITH

Cynthia Hobart Lindsay

PROLOGUE BY

Jack Benny

SIMON AND SCHUSTER · NEW YORK · 1955

LIBRARY OF CONGRESS CATALOG CARD NUMBER: 55-10045
MANUFACTURED IN THE UNITED STATES OF AMERICA
BY KINGSPORT PRESS, INC., KINGSPORT, TENN.

Contents

Contents

A section of illustrations will be found following page XIV.

Prologue

MY NAME is Jack Benny. I am an actor, a comedian, and a frustrated violinist. I am not a writer. I have a bunch of fellows who generally do this for me very well. But this particular job I wanted to do myself because I am what you might call an authority on the subject. George Burns is my closest friend. He may deny this, but it's true.

As I say, it is difficult for me to express myself in writing, for usually when I'm on-stage I emphasize a joke or story by pausing and looking at the audience. As I cannot very well do this with you readers, I thought I might use a device to indicate a pause.

Like this: Now about George Burns: I haven't read the book yet, but I know what's in it. It's an old story to me, with a few new twists. George never tells a story the same way twice. This is to lull you into a false sense of security so you won't think you've heard it before and stop him. Knowing George as well as I do, I could almost have written this book myself. *Almost*, meaning that I probably should have. Some of the episodes I am sure are true. Some of them will have a basis of truth and then will develop into the damnedest lies you have *ever* read. The reason for this is, he has told these stories so many times to the same people that he has to embellish each episode and find a new finish. Some of the stories will be completely true, but they didn't happen to him; they happened to somebody else. George Burns is the greatest offstage actor I know. Sometimes at a party when he is telling a long story about me, he is so convincing that I have to take him in the other room and say, "Did that really happen to me?" He says, "Of course not. It was Harpo Marx, but Harpo *isn't* here and you *are*."

The things you will no doubt read about George's mother—and his eleven sisters and brothers—are true, because nobody could make up anything so fantastic. But the anecdotes you will read about me are the ones I told you will be basically true and then drift into fantasy.

I don't have to enumerate these lies about me specifically, because the truth will be brought out at the trial in case I have to sue him. You must remember I haven't read the book yet, but I have an attorney in the bullpen.

Even though this is an autobiography, he will naturally include his source of income. I am referring to his wife—Gracie Allen. I wouldn't be presumptuous enough to venture an opinion on whether the chapters on Gracie are true or not. That close a friend *I'm* not. But I'm sure they must be true, because Gracie, even though professionally a zany character, in real life is a very capable and intelligent woman and won't stand for any nonsense. She is also a deeply talented actress, has natural beauty and a wonderful sense of humor. If you think that's a prejudiced statement, you're right. Why? I also love her, that's why.

Then of course there are a few situations that are lies right from the chapter number. I know all this, and I repeat: I haven't read the book. I am going to read it as soon as I finish the prologue. As a matter of fact, if I make the prologue long enough, Simon and Schuster may prefer it to the book—and with my usual business acumen, I can either sell it to them or peddle it elsewhere.

The book should be very interesting because in his short life (when wearing his toupee he's two years younger than I am) George has known everybody from Al Jolson to Al Capone. I wouldn't be surprised if he was still corresponding with Valeska Surat, Judge Crater, Powers Elephants, Lefty Louie, The Avon Comedy Four, Gyp the Blood, Flipper the Seal, and the end girl in Jesse Lasky's Redheads. Oh brother, the stories George tells about her—but that's another book.

As comedians George and I have something in common. Neither of us was discovered by Gus Edwards or Eddie Cantor, and our careers didn't start at Grossinger's. We came up the hard way, and knowing each other didn't make it any easier.

Of course, George had it real tough. Some people are born with a silver spoon in their mouth. George had a cigar.

In conclusion let me say this about George Burns: I love the guy. I have a reputation for being his easiest audience. I make constant resolutions that I'm not going to laugh at him any more—the hell with it. Then I'll walk into a party and he'll flick cigar ashes on the lapel of my new two-hundred-and-fifty-dollar suit, or he'll point at me in Romanoff's Restaurant and say, "Mr. Benny will take the check," and I'm gone again. What a clown!

However, I must say that of all the people I know, he has the finest qualities a man can possess. He is meticulous in his work. He is creative. He is generous to his enemies and magnanimous to his friends. To coin someone else's phrase, "He is a gentleman and a scholar."

So even though I am as big a liar as he is, I am proud to have him as my closest friend.

Now read the book and enjoy yourself. I am sure you will find it the kind of book you can't put down. I know I won't be able to. At three cents a day from the lending library I find myself a very fast reader.

JACK BENNY

Illustration Section

The Pee Wee Quartette. Left to right: George, Heshy Weinberger, Moish Friedman (he posed for Toda, who couldn't be located for the picture), and Mortzy Weinberger.

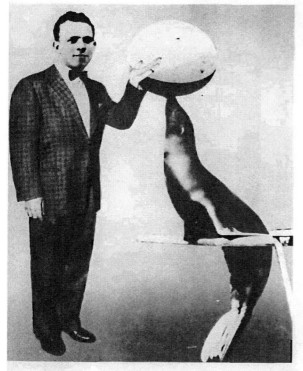

**EARLY
PROFESSIONAL
LIFE**

George and Flipper in the very early act, "Flipper and Friend."

"Larry and Co." From left to right: Gracie's sister Hazel, Larry Reilly, Gracie, and sister Bessie.

Gracie, when she was with Larry Reilly.

The picture of Gracie that appeared in the front of the theater during the run of *Lambchops*.

George in *Lambchops*. Another front-of-theater picture.

George and Gracie together in *Lambchops*.

Benny Fields, Blossom Seely, Gracie,
and George.

George, at about the time of
Lambchops.

Backstage at the Palace. From left to right: George, Gracie, Eddie Cantor, George Jessel, and Janet Reed. *Photo by White Studio.*

George and Gracie with Mary Boland and W. C. Fields in the Paramount picture *Six of a Kind.*

THE FAMILY

Gracie as a baby.

George and Gracie in 1934. "We were doing pretty well. I can tell by the dress."

Gracie with Sandra as a baby.

An early picture with Sandra and Ronald.

The family without George.

Ronnie, Gracie, and
Sandra in 1953.

George and son.

Back row: Ronnie, Gracie, George. *Front row:* Sandra Burns Wilhoite holding Laurie, and her husband, Jim.

Feasting from left to right: Danny Kaye, William Paley, Gracie, a Mr. Jack Benny, George Jessel, and George.

Author Burns and
authoress Lindsay.

George with a Mr. Jack
Benny in Hawaii.

Gracie explaining politics to Senator Alben Barkley.

Gracie (for President) throws her hat into the ring.

George and Gracie (Romeo and Juliet) backstage at a benefit with Isabel Jewell.

George, Frank Sinatra, a Mr. Jack Benny, Groucho Marx, and Danny Kaye.

George with a Mr. Jack
Benny acting as a
substitute Gracie on TV.

Bing Crosby, a Mr. Jack
Benny, and George.

Backstage at a benefit: Eddie Cantor, a Mr. Jack Benny, and George.

At a testimonial dinner for a real old-timer called Jack Benny: William Paley, George Jessel, George, the guest of honor, Fred Allen, and Adlai Stevenson.

I LOVE HER,
THAT'S WHY!

The Pee Wee Quartette

1

So she puts the salt in the pepper shaker and the pepper in the salt shaker because then if she gets mixed up she's right. And she shortens the electric cords on the lamps and irons in the house to save electricity. And she always drives with the emergency brake on so if she runs into an emergency she's ready for it. Of course that's the character she plays.

I must run into about a dozen people a week who always ask the same question and always get the same answer. Question: "George, you've been married all these years. How can you take it? Why do you—?" Answer: I love her. That's why.

I guess you might say my life never really began until I met her. Of course, there were a few things— like being born. This happened January 20, 1896, at 95 Pitt Street, New York City. (And I'd appreciate it if you wouldn't let this get around—keep it under your hat. I tell everybody I'm fifty-eight.) They named me Nathan Birnbaum. When I was born I was the youngest in my family, but this position didn't last long. There were more to come. Before Mother got through there were twelve—seven girls and five boys. If I can remember the order, they came like this: Morris, Annie, Isadore, Esther, Sarah, Sadie, Mamie, Goldie, Nathan (that's me), Sammy, Theresa, and Willie.

I can't remember much about the first two years of my life, except that I had long curls. In fact, I had them until I was five because we didn't have the price of a haircut. When I was five we moved to 259 Rivington Street, a four-story building with four apartments on each floor and a butcher shop and grocery store downstairs. Mother was always hiding us from the welfare people because they didn't seem to think our apartment was big enough for fourteen people. I don't know why—we had three rooms. We had a front room with two windows, a kitchen with a skylight, and a bedroom with no windows at all. No bathroom. We took baths in the kitchen tub. There was only enough hot water for one tubful, so the oldest got the first bath and the rest of us took turns, according to age, in the same water. You can imagine what it was like when they got to me. I was cleaner when I got in.

The other plumbing conveniences were in an outhouse in the back yard three stories below. Sometimes this was a problem. All the lights, which were gas, were turned off at ten o'clock. Any one of us kids who had to go to the bathroom after that was followed by a rapid fire of shouted conversation from my mother standing in the hall as we made our way

4

down the stairs and out into the night. The minute we hit the yard, she switched positions and yelled out the window at us until we started back up the stairs. This was so we shouldn't be scared of the dark. It made us a little self-conscious, though, because not only everybody in our apartment house but all the others on the block knew what we were doing.

At five I was getting the scent of show business. We had an organ-grinder on our street—with a strictly second-class organ, very flat. The men who owned the good ones worked Second Avenue. We only got the organ-grinders that were breaking in, and why they bothered to come around I'll never know. Nobody had any pennies to throw them. Anyway, it was music of a sort, and all the little girls in the block would dance around him. I did too. I had a Spanish number I did, and if I say so myself, I was very graceful. The people clapped for me and I got my first feel of an audience.

At seven I found out I had teeth. Up to that point I was in the gravy age. It was like the tub routine. The way it worked out in our family was the older kids got the meat, the young ones the gravy. We didn't think the food was bad, because we had no basis of comparison; we thought it all tasted like that. Also at seven two very important things happened. My father died and I went into show business for real.

I tried other work first, anything I could get to help out, like selling papers, shining shoes, etc. Then with three other boys on the block I formed the Pee

I Love Her, That's Why!

Wee Quartette. I sang tenor, a boy called Toda the lead, Mortzy Weinberger sang baritone, and his brother Heshy, bass. I'll let you in on a secret: we didn't know how to sing harmony. We figured the kid who held his head highest was tenor, and so on down to the bass, who held his chin on his chest. We sang in yards and saloons and passed the hat afterward. We rotated the job of hat passer because we didn't trust each other. I guess we were right, because after every performance we searched the one with the hat and always found him with at least a dime in his mouth. I got so I was a pro—I could handle six or seven dimes and sing at the same time.

There were days when we couldn't collect a penny, and on those empty-hat days we would go up on the roofs of the apartment houses and, lying on our stomachs, hang a long wire over the ledge. The curved end of the wire we hooked over Seltzer bottles that people had left out on their fire escapes for collection, and pulled them up to the roof. There we broke off the lead tops, took them down to the basement, and building a fire under the top of an old milk can, melted them down. Lead was six cents a a pound at the time, and on a good day we could make a dollar. Split four ways, that gave us twenty-five cents apiece. To give you a rough idea how good the Pee Wee Quartette was, we went out seven days a week and six of them we melted lead. This is how I became a producer.

It was Lew Farley, the letter carrier on our block, who straightened us out on harmony. He would join us in the cellar of Rosenzweig's candy store at Columbia and Stanton, where we were working, and we worked and rehearsed at the same time. This wasn't as hard as it sounds, because our job didn't take much brain work. What we did was make the syrup for Mr. Rosenzweig's sodas. There were big vats of all flavors cooking, and mostly we just stirred. We worked from three to five every day and our pay was five cents apiece and all the soda we could drink—we would insist on plain. We were full of syrup. One day Lew Farley was directing us, and Toda, our lead singer, backed into a vat of chocolate syrup. Although this was painful, we finished our number—we'd already heard that "show must go on" line. When we finished, we pulled Toda out, cleaned him up, and bottled the syrup. Mr. Rosenzweig never found out, and as far as we know there were no complaints from the customers.

I guess you might say everybody in our neighborhood was Jewish. There may have been a few who weren't but I certainly don't remember any. All the kids went to P.S. 22, and we were always involved in a serious gang war with the students of the nearby parochial school. The war generally opened in the winter with somebody throwing a snowball that he had carefully frozen first. Somebody else's head was then cracked open and we were off to the races. These were not kidding wars, with broken bottles as weapons and the lids off washtubs for shields.

When we really got going, nothing could stop us except the appearance of another gang from Mangin Street. These kids were mostly Italian; they loved a fight, and when we had a good thing going they

7

would be afraid they were missing something and try to get into the act. We weren't having it, though; it was our fight. We joined forces and drove the common enemy back behind his own lines. That was Mangin Street, and that was bad luck, because we had to cross it every day. It worked this way: The ice company delivered ice to the stores in the neighborhood early every morning. Any left over, they sold for five cents a cake. A bunch of us kids from P.S. 22 and from the parochial school would get up at five in the morning, tear across town, fighting all the way, get to the ice truck, panting, and then stand in a quiet and complete truce in line, waiting for a cake of ice, because this was not only business, this was family. For five cents you could get the cake of ice, put it on a wagon and quarter it. You then sold three pieces for five cents apiece and had one for your own icebox. You had a ten-cent profit and were helping out—that is, if you made it back across Mangin Street with the ice intact. With any luck, you could supply your family, make your profit, and get a hole in the head before school started.

We had a way of getting in a food supply, too, that was pretty clever. We cut the bottoms out of the pockets of our coats, then we would get the attention of a pushcart peddler by pointing to something high up on the cart and saying, "How much are those?" As he looked up we took the non-pointing hand, thrust it through the pocket, out through the lining, and snatched up whatever fruit was within reach. Pretty soon, though, the peddlers got on to this gag, and the police were always looking for somebody who'd tried it. The kids didn't get caught often because they had a great hiding place. All the apartments had the drinking water supply in tanks on the roofs. At the approach of a policeman the kid being chased climbed up the tank and would hang by his hands with the rest of him in the water until danger passed. My mother saved me from the law, and our water supply from possible pollution, by a simple device: she sewed up my pockets.

I'll never forget one guy in the neighborhood, about this time. His name was Harry Mittleman. He was about twenty-four, and he was a sort of a dope—the kind who would say, "I bet I can eat fifteen corned-beef sandwiches without stopping." Somebody would say, "I'll bet you couldn't do it if they cut the bread sideways"—that would make the sandwiches twice as big—and he'd say, very dignified, "I wouldn't take the bet if the bread wasn't cut sideways."

Mittleman was just as strong as he was stupid. I never saw such a powerful guy. And he loved to show off. He was old enough to know better, but I guess you might call him a sort of senile delinquent. Anyway, if there were any girls around he had to prove how strong he was. In the summer there were always some sitting out on their front steps to get themselves cooled off or the boys warmed up. There were also always horses and wagons parked by the curb. Harry would spot a bunch of girls, pretend he didn't see them, walk over to the curb, put both shoulders under a horse and lift it right up off the ground—all four feet. Then, as if it was nothing, he'd drop the horse and walk slowly away—whistling. The horse was always very surprised; the girls were not. They were sick of that trick—they saw it all the time.

One night Mittleman was in Huber's museum on Fourteenth Street, which was a sort of a combination vaudeville and freak show. The strong man had got himself a smashing climax worked out for his act; he passed a horseshoe out to the audience, to prove it was real iron, and barked, "Ladies and gentlemen, I will now do something never attempted on any stage: I shall take that horseshoe and I shall straighten it out with my bare hands." At this point the horseshoe had been passed to Mittleman, who stood up, bent the horseshoe into a straight line, and said, "Like this?" The strong man left the stage and I guess he's still looking for a new finish.

The highest ambition of the Pee Wee Quartette and its maestro, Lew Farley, was to get booked for amateur night at the Cannon Street picture house. There was always a long line of kids outside the theater, because children's tickets were two for a nickel and everybody was always holding out to get somebody else to pay the three-cent part. Finally it got so there were fifty kids standing outside with two cents each. Lew finally got us booked and we were torn between being thrilled to death and scared to death, not of the audience, but of the men in the front row whose job was to get you off the stage if you laid an egg. They didn't use a hook the way most theaters did then; they used a long pole with a hoop on the end. They would drop this over you like a butterfly net and drag you over the footlights. You

10

didn't just have to be able to sing—you had to know how to break falls, too.

We didn't know it, but this night we were in worse danger than getting the hoop. There was a girl on just before us who was billed as Red Ribbons. It was easy to tell why, she had them all over her head—lots of curls and lots of ribbons, all red. It seems she was keeping steady company with a gentleman named Crazo—not one of the Marx brothers, but a gangster of some reputation on the East Side. He was a little bit nuts—no, wait a minute, as long as I'm telling it I might as well tell the truth, he was *real* nuts. Now this night he was in the audience rooting for his girl, and he had let it be noised around that he would "get" anyone who took first prize away from her. Even so, we didn't hold back; this was our big chance and we weren't about to muff it. We were right in the middle of a number and it looked as if we might be going for first prize. People were throwing nickels and dimes on the stage, and things were looking great when suddenly I got it. Now I don't know if you've ever been hit in the head by four dollars and sixty cents' worth of nickels, but I have. Crazo had bunched up that many coins and hurled them with full force at my head. I don't know why me. Maybe he just didn't like tenors.

I didn't think of fainting—there was too much money on the stage—and I wasn't going to be unconscious when it was picked up. We each got a dollar and fifteen cents in red nickels—by this time I was bleeding heavily—and we also won first prize of five dollars.

Drunk with our success, we decided to go out and

celebrate. However, we had to control that "meet you at Sardi's" feeling because we heard that Crazo was waiting at the stage door for us. It was midnight when we got up courage to leave, and there was no sign of him—he was probably busy consoling Red Ribbons.

We went to Berkowitz's Restaurant on Houston Street where you got steak, potatoes, cole slaw, dessert, coffee, and all the bread and butter you could eat, for twenty-five cents. The steak was very large and very thin, in fact it was so thin it hung over the edge of the plate so you couldn't see the waiter's hand when he brought it in. We ate a colossal meal, relived our triumph, and nobody thought how late it was. I got home about one o'clock and found my whole family waiting for me. I couldn't see why they were worried and mad. I was seven years old and able to take care of myself.

My sister Sadie was the maddest. She had been out on the front steps looking for me, and her boy friend Louie was with her. They didn't see any point in wasting the time, so while they were looking they did a bit of smootching, too. They were sitting on the stoop enjoying themselves when one of the neighbors' kids who was sleeping on the fire escape rolled off and fell into my sister Sadie's lap. Sadie took the little boy out of her lap and got off Louie's and carried him upstairs. When I came in my mother cried, and bandaged my head, and yelled at me, and kissed me, and said why didn't I go to school like a good boy instead of fooling around with actors. Everybody talked and nobody listened. Then I reached in my pocket and took out two dollars' worth of nickels. It was good for a moment of respectful silence and a round of applause.

Thus established in show business, it remained for me to get a name that would look better in lights than Nathan Birnbaum. I got the one I have by returning a favor to a friend. Abie Kaplan used to hang out in Hamilton Fish Park where all the great buck dancers started. I would watch the kids showing each other steps, and wish I could do it—I thought the Pee Wee Quartette could use a little dancing with its songs. Abie could do a time step and offered to teach me. I was so grateful that I offered to share with him my greatest secret and what I considered the finest invention since Edison's electric light. He accepted and we formed our alliance. The Burns Brothers coal yard was ten blocks from our house. When their trucks started out with a load of coal, we followed, and a couple of blocks from where they loaded, we opened the chute, let some coal drop onto the street, and shut the chute.

In those days boys wore knickers, which were a perfect garment for this work. We filled our pants with coal and walked home. There were very few who didn't know what we were doing, and one day as we walked stiff-legged down the street with our knickers bulging, the grocer watched us pass and said, "There go the Burns Brothers." The name stuck. So did the coal. Sammy, the brother who got the tub after me on the coal days, came out looking like end man in a minstrel show. Abie and I became partners. I became Nathan Burns, he became Al

Burns, and the Burns Brothers were in business.

The Burns Brothers' first engagement was at Seiden's Theater on Columbia Street. This was a picture house which ran vaudeville acts as well. There was a pool hall downstairs and it was difficult to hear either the vaudeville acts before the movie or the music accompanying the picture—the noise of the pool balls drowned out almost all other sounds. The movies were made as silent pictures, but by the time the Seidens, father and sons, finished with them they were anything but. I guess they figured competition was so great that they had better add something to get the customers in. So the three of them, Mr. Seiden, Joe, and Jack, stood behind the screen and talked for the actors. They had a few regular parts. Joe was always the girl, although he played other parts as well. Sometimes he'd get mixed up about what was going on. In *The Great Train Robbery*, William Farnum sounded a little like Mary Pickford.

The theater ran two vaudeville acts—one in Yiddish and one in English. The Burns Brothers' job was to handle the curtain. This took a bit of doing, because the curtain rolled from the bottom on a heavy wooden pole which was controlled by ropes on each side of the stage. Burns and Burns together weighed about 120 pounds and the pole weighed half again as much. We were able to get the curtain up twice without staggering, but if the act went over big and they took more than two curtain calls we were dead. One week Seiden booked a Yiddish sketch called "Religion Versus Love." The plot involved a

14

Gentile girl who wanted her Jewish lover to give up his religion and marry her. The smash finish of this act was when the boy cried, "No! A Jew I was born, and a Jew I shall die!" Well, this was good for about fifteen curtain calls, and with each we got weaker and the curtain got lower. For the last bow the actors were lying on their stomachs.

It was about six months from the start of the Burns Brothers routine that I got the rest of my name. I had an older brother whose name was Isadore H. Birnbaum. That H was for free; he stuck it in himself; it didn't stand for anything; he just thought it sounded good. His friends, who were fond of him and seemed to need a nickname for him, called him George—not Izzy, but George. Well, I thought this brother was quite a feller. I was crazy about him. If George was a good enough name for him, it was good enough for me. So I became George.

At seven, George Burns was a dedicated man. He lived for his art. There was no time for anything else. Sure there were girls. I remember one—she was a skater in the park, a beautiful skater and a beautiful girl. She had big blue eyes, tight black corkscrew curls, and on Sunday she wore white Russian boots. She had everything—everything that is, except the most important thing in my life: she couldn't sing harmony.

Twenty years later I met Gracie.

2

AT NINE I was a first-rate student of the buck
and wing at Hamilton Fish Park. I must have ex-
pended my scholarly abilities there, because I wasn't
doing so well at P.S. 22. In fact, I guess you would
say I wasn't doing at all well. By this time I had a
new name. It was Tootchoo. The name came from
the fact that in the summer I went barefooted, therefore I was called No Shoes. Naturally, when winter
came, and I was given a pair, I became Two Shoes
—it was easy for that to slip into Tootchoo. One particular pair of shoes became my most valued posses-
sion. They had wooden soles and were given me by a
buck dancer in Hamilton Fish Park who thought
they were worn out. He was wrong. I wore them for
years, which was no trick, because when he gave
them to me I wore a size six and the shoes were nine
and a half. They didn't look neat but they made up
for it numerous ways. I learned to dance in them,
and like the Greek fellow who learned to talk with
pebbles in his mouth, if I could dance in those shoes

without dancing out of them I could dance in anything.

They also saved my sister Sarah a lot of sleep. She was the family worrier, and as we used to rehearse in the park until eleven or twelve at night she always waited up for me. I walked home *clunkety-clunkety-clunk* in those shoes, and she could go to sleep six blocks earlier because she could hear me coming. Later, when the shoes finally wore out, we worked out another system. A few blocks from home, I walked in the gutter and kept lighting matches which I threw in the air. Sarah could see them from the window, know I was safe, and go to sleep.

What with not getting home from rehearsals until about midnight, and playing hookey constantly for engagements of the Pee Wee Quartette, my school work suffered so severely that my teacher, Miss Klein, came to talk to my mother. As I heard her ask our neighbor, Mrs. Sapin, where we lived, I ducked under the bed. Mamma saw me go. She knew Miss Klein and she also knew why she was at the door. She stepped over my brother Willie who was playing on the floor with a piece of coal (these were our rich days—we each had our own piece to play with) and let Miss Klein in. Miss Klein was nice but firm. I couldn't hear everything she said, but I did get that I was too busy telling jokes in class to learn anything, that my attendance was not poor—it was poverty-stricken, that I was capable of doing better, and that I had better do better because I couldn't do worse.

I Love Her, That's Why!

In the middle of the discussion the door opened and my brother Sammy came in. I thought it was Miss Klein going out, and hollered, "Mamma, is she gone already?" My mother's performance for Miss Klein should have netted her an Academy Award. What a straight man! She yelled, "So that's where you are, playing hookey!" She dragged me out by the collar and glared at me. Miss Klein said, "Well, I guess you can handle this. I'll be going."

"Handle it!" said my mother. "With a stick I'll handle it!" She was holding me so that my toes barely touched the floor. She closed the door on Miss Klein and dropped me. My shoes made so much noise that Mrs. Goldberg from the apartment below beat on the floor with a broom.

"Nat," my mother said, "I want to talk to you, Nat, and I want you should listen. Keep close to me, because I can't be stopping my work to talk." She was kneading the *challe*, a Jewish bread made with eggs, except in our case we didn't have any eggs. I watched her with interest, as on Fridays I always was the one to take it to the bakery to be baked. Saturday being a Jewish holiday, my mother had to bake a big enough loaf to last over until Sunday, and a loaf of that size wouldn't fit in our oven. Transporting the loaf was my job, because it seemed to come back bigger when I took it. Mother didn't know I swapped ours with Mrs. Sapin's from next door. This way we ended with an eight-pound loaf instead of the six-pound loaf my mother started with—also, sometimes Mrs. Sapin had eggs in hers.

Well, I knew Mamma was mad this day, because she gave the bread to Sammy to take to the bakery.

Her running lecture on the importance of education never ceased as she swept, cooked, dusted, took care of the little children, washed the clothes and put them in the basket. I helped her carry the basket up to the roof with a heavy heart, because I knew what my punishment was going to be. Someone had to sit with the clothes until they dried, otherwise other children stole them and sold them to the ragman. It was a lonely job up there with nobody to talk to, and it was a damp day, so it looked like a long stretch. Mamma put her end of the heavy basket down and finished her lecture simultaneously. She drew her arm across her perspiring forehead and said, "So hang them up—and don't move from here until they're dry. Now remember what I said, and in conclusion, please, Nat, be a good boy." She started down the stairs, then turned back and called, "And about Miss Klein, I am not going to punish you, because you're doing the right thing. Grow up to be a dope. There's a lot of money in it." The last three minutes of her lecture she delivered with a mouthful of clothespins: this was the first double-talk routine I ever heard.

I had a lot of time to think, up there that day, and the next morning I started off for school like a good boy. On the way I met Mortzy Weinberger who said, "Where you been? There's an affair at the Second Avenue Rathskeller tonight—a smoker and stag. If we can try out right now they'll use the Pee Wee

Quartette." I missed school that day, but the next day, as a peace offering, instead of an apple, I took Miss Klein a pretzel from the rathskeller.

In the long run, it was my training in the theater that got me out of the fourth grade. The school play was "The Life of Peter Stuyvesant," and I was playing Peter Stuyvesant—naturally. The finale of this opus was supposed to be that Uncle Sam came out on the stage and said to the audience, "We will now all stand and sing 'My Country 'Tis of Thee.' Now *everybody* sing!" Well, I was the only one in the school who had an Uncle Sam suit. This put me in a bargaining position. I said the school could borrow it, but only if my sister Theresa played Uncle Sam—not that she wanted to play Uncle Sam, in fact she hated the idea; she didn't think she looked pretty in a beard. However, I insisted, and play it she did. She was a very unhappy Uncle Sam.

I gave my performance of Peter Stuyvesant everything. One of my legs was wrapped in gauze to make it look like a wooden leg; by the time we got to the "My Country 'Tis of Thee" part, the gauze had unraveled all over the stage. I tripped and fell and pulled Uncle Sam down with me. After my performance I limped for two days so everyone would know I'd played Stuyvesant. I'm not saying it was my masterful rendition of the part that got me out of the fourth. It may have been the fact that Miss Klein was interested in a gentleman who liked to dance and she couldn't dance. I gave her lessons. She got the feller and I got passing grades.

At this time the Pee Wee Quartette had a splendid secret source of income. We were working at Rosenzweig's candy store, stealing the bags he sold the candy in and selling them to the rival concern across the street. We had wanted to go on the road to Coney Island but the streetcar ride cost five cents apiece and we couldn't afford it. Therefore this bag business was just what we needed. We saved enough from the profits to strike out. We were not a smash hit in Coney Island—we had forgotten that bathing suits don't have pockets. I thought for a moment that we were in luck, because I ran into my Uncle Frank. He was a wonderful man. I'll never forget his sense of humor. One day a boy came into his butcher shop and said, "Do you want to buy a cat?" He said, "Business is so bad I'll take a half a cat." He couldn't help us, though. He didn't have any money either. Well, we went from beach to beach singing our hearts out, because people kept applauding. But the hat came back full of nothing but sand and tokens for some of the concessions in Steeplechase Park. So we took a ride on the roller coaster, which was great on empty stomachs.

By nightfall our situation was desperate and we knew we had to strike out for fresh territory. At that hour of the evening the lights of Bergen Beach looked pretty close, so we tossed a token and started out. The lights were deceiving. Bergen Beach was several miles away across a swamp. We waded halfway across the swamp before we found out that it was infested with giant water rats. Now we were a brave bunch of boys who had been known to walk right up and bark at a cocker spaniel, but when these things attacked us we were plain scared. They must have been Bergen Beach rats that heard us sing, because they chased us all the way back to Coney Island.

We arrived there at two in the morning, hungry, cold, tired, and frightened, just in time to see the last streetcar pulling out. We jumped on, hoping to make enough out of a couple of songs to pay our carfare. We opened with one of our peppiest numbers, "Syncopation Rules the Nation," and the people had to lean over to hear us, we were so weak. I passed the hat, and the first man I approached turned out to be my brother Morris. He was with a girl, telling her what a big man he was when I appeared. I looked like the son of a tramp comedian. He was terribly embarrassed and was real angry with me. Well, he paid our fares. There were plenty of seats, but I rode home standing up. A few blocks from home Morris, who knew my sister Sarah would be hanging out the window looking for me, started lighting matches and throwing them in the air to cue her that we were on the way so she could go to sleep. Morris' girl watched him do this for about five blocks but didn't say anything.

When we got home Morris made the girl wait downstairs while he took me up to Mamma. She and all my sisters were pacing up and down the aisles between the mattresses on the floor where the young kids were asleep. They slept sideways so more of them could get on, but they didn't mind, because Mamma always told us how lucky we were we didn't have to sleep on the floor like the poor kids. Morris joined the rest in a few minutes of yelling at me, and by the time he went down after the girl, she was gone. Harry Mittleman had lifted a horse for her, and what with match-throwing and horse-lifting she got the impression there was something peculiar about our neighborhood.

The fact that we flopped in Coney Island didn't break the spirit of the Pee Wee Quartette. Our next job was a great success, because we had what in these days of television you call a "captive audience." We went to work in an establishment owned by two gangsters called "Big Puss" and "Little Puss." It was a saloon which ran bootleg prize fights in the rear. Our assignment was to stand by, and when the police raided the place the fighters ducked out of the ring and hid under the tables, and we jumped into the ring and started to sing. We always sang very fast, because the minute the cops left we got thrown out. Our timing became so good that we could finish a number just as the cops finished their inspection. On a good night, when they lined up everybody and frisked them to see if they carried guns, we could get through all of "Roll Those Bones" and "Mary Ann, Mary Ann, Mary Sat in a Corner" and a chorus of "Dorondo, You're a Gooda-for-Not" before we were pulled off. We were getting two dollars a night for this front work and were very well satisfied, when Big Puss called me over to him and said, "Tootchoo, I've got a little job for you."

I was proud, because Big Puss was a very famous gangster. "Tomorrow," he said, "you go to this address on Pitkin Avenue in Brownsville. Across the street is a restaurant with a shoeshine stand in front of it. I'm going into the restaurant to kill a man. When you see me come out and get up on the stand to get my shine, you get up beside me and I'll hand you this gun. Take the elevated back here and leave the gun in the poolroom for me. Be at Pitkin Avenue at exactly five minutes to three."

This was big time, and I hated to have to turn him down. I said, "Gee, Mr. Big Puss, I'd love to do it, but I've got a date with Lew Farley at three o'clock at Rosenzweig's. He's teaching the Pee Wee Quartette harmony on 'When Uncle Joe Plays a Rag on His Old Banjo' and I've got to be there because that's one of the hit numbers of the Arlington Comedy Four."

Big Puss looked at me as if I was nuts. He must have been disappointed in me, because the next time he held the bootleg fights we were replaced by a harmonica player. So you see, if it hadn't been for my love of harmony I might have amounted to something.

In the summer we devoted much of our time to healthy outdoor sports. Two of the boyish activities which gave us the most pleasure were hat snatching and hydrant lifting. A great deal of imagination and brain work went into these games and they gave us excellent training in histrionics and scene shifting. The first worked this way: we waited outside the drugstore where the only telephone in the neighborhood was located. We tied a string to a piece of coal, threw it over the telephone wire, removed the coal, and attached a metal clamp to the end of the string. As soon as it was dark we hid in the hallway next to the drugstore, and when a man walked by with a straw hat on we sneaked up behind him and clamped the string to the back of his hat. One of us then pulled the string and the hat rose neatly in the air. We could manage to keep the hat just out of a man's reach long enough to get a lot of laughs and learn some new words.

The other game was a killer. This started with a burlap sack. We put the sack over a fire hydrant, tied it carefully and tightly with string, and one of us, generally me, because all tenors cry easily, would stand next to the hydrant sobbing pathetically. It was never long before some passerby with a kind heart would stop and say, "What's the matter, little boy?" Giving it everything, I sobbed, "I've got to take this home and I can't get it on my back." The good Samaritan would invariably lean over and give it a good hoist. When they carried the man into the drugstore we played other games. I told you this was a killer.

About this time I got religion. Previously I had had no time for it. Not that my mother didn't try. We were an orthodox Jewish family and observed all the rules. That was one of the reasons the *challe* had to be baked on Friday night, because the baker had to be paid, and from sundown Friday until sundown Saturday it is against the Jewish religion to carry money in your pockets. This never presented much of a problem. There was hardly ever any money to

25

carry. Mamma tried to get all of us to take a proper interest in our faith, and all of my brothers and sisters have maintained it until this day.

As far as I was concerned, though, I was always, right from the start, too interested in show business to be interested in anything else. Later in life I kind of made up a religion for myself. I think everybody's religion is a good one as long as they don't start telling anybody else it's the only one. You take us, for instance. Gracie is a Catholic and a good one. Both of our children are Catholics. My daughter Sandra has a new baby who's Catholic, and Sandra's husband is an Episcopalian. The way I see it, their only problem is, she'll have to go to early mass in order to get back in time to baby sit while he catches the eleven o'clock service at his church.

I guess if you tried to boil down the way I feel about the religion I invented, it's this: I keep my word. I stayed with one agency for twenty-five years without ever signing a contract. I mind my own business; people can do what they want—it's no skin off my back. Gracie is always complaining that I never bring her any gossip from the studio or the club. I guess I just don't hear it, that's all. I never tell a lie. Well, that is, I never tell a lie without saying right afterward, "That's a lie." Sometimes it just makes a better story if you dress it up a little. I don't steal. Not anymore, I mean. I'm not hungry anymore. I respected my mother and my father. One of the things that makes me happiest is that Mamma lived to catch us at the Palace. I love my family and try to be a good husband and father. I also love our

poodle, Mousie, and I'm kind to other animals even
if they aren't poodles. I just said I made up this religion, but now that I come to think of it, I wouldn't
be a bit surprised if I'd heard it somewhere before.

But this is getting away from the subject. Anyway, when I was nine, I joined a church. One Friday
I came home and said, "Mamma, I'm an Episper-
terian."

"That's nice," she said, "take the *challe* to the
baker."

"But, Mamma," I said, "all the members of the
Pee Wee Quartette had to join the church before we
could be in the Wanamaker choir contest next
Wednesday."

"So?" she said. "And what kind of a contest is
that?"

I answered, "It's a contest for choirs and they
have prizes for the best choir. We went to this
church on Rivington Street. I'm not sure about that
name—"

"It's probably the Presbyterian," Mamma said.
"So what happened?"

"So this church is very poor—I guess most everybody is a Catholic or a Jew—and they don't have a
choir, and they said we could be their choir in the
contest if we joined up."

"So fine," Mamma said; "Wednesday you're a
Presbyterian, until then you're a Jew, and if you
don't stop talking, that *challe* is going to rise while
you carry it to the baker."

The John Wanamaker choir contest was held on a
farm in New Jersey which was also the training

camp for one of the greatest fighters of the day, Sam Langford, and his sparring partner, Joe Jeanette. The whole day was glorious. It opened with an exhibition match by Langford and Jeanette. Then came the choir contest, and the Pee Wee Presbyterian Quartette came in first. And what do you think the prize was? As if the honor wasn't enough, the first prize was, we were allowed to feel Sam Langford's muscles. I came to the conclusion that he could lift a horse with Harry Mittleman on it.

Being a Presbyterian didn't last long. I had a good friend, an Italian boy named Louis Linelli. He was a Catholic. The day he was confirmed, his grandfather, who owned a lot of pushcarts, gave him a gold watch. That did it. I went home to Mamma. "Mamma," I said, "I changed my religion again."

"So?" she said, looking up from the washtub. "And what are you today?" "A Catholic." She said, "Fine. Take the wash up on the roof and when it dries you can come back and tell me about it."

Two and a half hours later when I returned she said, "Nu? So tell me, what made you a Catholic today?" "You know Louis Linelli whose grandfather owns all the pushcarts," I said. "Well, he was just confirmed." "Confirmed?" "*Bar mitzvahed.*" "Oh." "And his grandfather gave him a solid-gold watch. Now I'm going to be confirmed, and maybe his grandfather will give me a gold watch, too." "That's nice," Mamma said. "Maybe he will. Aaron Moskowitz was just *bar mitzvahed* and all he got was a bicycle pump."

Two weeks later I had another report for my

mother. The Weinberger boys brought me the news while I was melting down some Seltzer-bottle tops. I ran home to Mamma. "Mamma," I said, "guess what? Louis Linelli's grandfather caught him stealing off of one of his own pushcarts, and he got so mad he took the watch back. Now Louis's so mad he's decided to be a Jew."

When I was thirteen I was *bar mitzvahed*. I didn't get a bicycle pump, but I did get to be a baritone. This meant I had to break with the Pee Wee Quartette. It was a sad parting but unavoidable. They already had a baritone. As my voice dropped, my interest in the opposite sex mounted. I was taking notice of one girl in particular. In fact, all the boys in the neighborhood noticed her. Her name was Millie Hart, and she was something. I did everything but stand on my head to get her attention; in fact, I think I did stand on my head. A whole bunch of us, Millie included, used to go to Coney Island in the summer. I had it on the rest of the boys because I knew how to entertain. Millie thought I was a scream. I danced and sang and told jokes, and it was great, because the beach was so crowded my audience couldn't walk out on me. But fate kept me from the girl of my dreams, because I worked so hard, and it was so hot, and I sweat so much that, by the time I had showered and cleaned up, Millie had gone home with Marcy Klauber. I lost the girl, but my efforts were not entirely wasted, because I improved my timing.

Fourteen years later I met Gracie.

My Brush with the Garment Industry

3

WHEN I reached the age of thirteen my legs began to straighten out. Up to that time, like all the kids in the neighborhood, they were bowed from lack of proper food and vitamins. In fact, bowlegs were so common that once, when a kid moved into the neighborhood with straight legs, we all thought he was a sissy. Malnutrition had everybody a little on the weak side but the diet deficiency seemed to affect boys and girls differently. My sisters' legs were straight, but my sisters fainted all the time. If anything ever happened to upset my sister Sarah, she fainted. The minute my sister Sadie saw her, she'd wobble a little and fall down beside her. It was a kind of sympathy faint. My sister Mamie revived them. Then Sarah and Sadie would get up off the floor while my sister Goldie was reviving Mamie. This anecdote is dressed up a little, but it's basically true.

Anyway, I was now a baritone with straight legs and a few card tricks, and business started to pick up. I was entertaining one night at an affair, and was discovered. I was singing, "I Am Tying the Leaves So They Won't Fall Down, So Daddy Won't Go Away." This was a long title and a long song, but I was young and had nothing else to do. At the end of the song, a man named Mac Fry introduced himself to me and offered me a job in his act, "Mac Fry and Company." I was the "and Company." The act was a tour de force (my collaborator loves this expression) for me. It gave me an opportunity to sing, dance, and act. We opened at a burlesque house in Brooklyn that ran vaudeville acts during the intermission. We did a sketch in which I played a shoeshine boy. I was supposed to be very ragged, and family conditions were such that I wore the same clothes on-stage and off. The opening of the act found me offstage singing, "Shine, shine, five cents a shine; my name is Teddy, and I'm always ready. My blacking is new, my polish is fine, so won't you step up?—it's five cents a shine."

All through my song, Mac Fry sat at a desk, on-stage, listening to me. At the end of the song, I stuck my head on and said, "Shine, Boss?" Now, I won't bore you with the plot—it was tough enough on that audience—but briefly, the action was, he said yes he'd have a shine, then he offered me a job, and explained to the audience that he was going to test my honesty by a series of clever devices. He left the stage saying, "There's fifty thousand dollars in that drawer—guard it with your life." I said, "I'm so happy that I got a job, I think I'll sing a song." And did. It was, "Always Think of Mother." A very sad song. This gave Fry time to make his first change. He came back three separate times in different disguises to try and get me to help him steal the money. Each time I said no. The final time, he appeared in a beard, forced me to give him the money. I opened the drawer of the desk, found a gun, pulled it out and said, "So you want the money, eh? Well, take that!" Mr. Fry would pull his beard off and shout, "Don't shoot! I'm your boss!" Then the curtain came down and it stayed down. It was very hard to tell whether the sketch was good or bad, because while we were on nobody watched us. Half of the house was out smoking, and the fellows sitting near the runway were cleaning their glasses, and I guess the rest of them were mad at us because they didn't like the prizes they found in their cracker-jack boxes.

My family didn't believe that I was a dramatic actor, so I brought the gun home to prove it. And the truant officer was waiting for me. He took me to the principal's office where they found the gun on me, and I was in real trouble. They didn't understand about props, and I had a hard time explaining, because I used to stammer.

Our next engagement was at the Windsor Theater on the Bowery. The headliner was a prize fighter named Young O'Leary. You might say we all gave a farewell performance, because they were tearing the theater down while the show was going on. We opened on Thursday. Friday, when we came off, the plumbing was gone. Saturday matinee, we went to our dressing rooms and they were gone. Saturday night, we played in an open air theater as the roof was gone. Sunday, after our last performance, we went to the manager's office to get paid, and it was gone. So was the manager. We never did get paid.

That was the end of Fry and Company. I continued to rehearse in Hamilton Fish Park and under the Williamsburg Bridge. I wasn't looking my best, as I had holes in my shoes, and a hole in the front of my mouth where someone had knocked out one of my teeth by hitting me on the back of the head while I was drinking at a water fountain. For the next two years I was a small smiler.

There was an act which rehearsed in the Park that I thought was about the greatest thing I'd ever seen. It was called "Brown and Williams, Fifteen Minutes of Singing, Dancing, and Roller Skating." This act broke up, and Sam Brown, who had been watching me dance, asked me to join up with him. The first thing he did was change my name to Williams. We became Brown and Williams. We opened the act with a soft-shoe dance, then a single song by me, "Augustus J. McCan Was a Henpecked Married Man." This was to give Brown time to put on his skates. He did some fancy skating while I put mine on, and we did a double buck dance on roller skates to "Shuffles and Taps." We finished with an eccentric number with frock coats and high hats to "Chicken Reel."

Our first booking was at the Imperial Theater on 116th Street. In those days the theaters were built so that the stage slanted down toward the audience instead of the audience being slanted upward away from the stage, the way it is now. I didn't know this, and when I was on skates I kept sliding down hill into the footlights, and Brown kept pulling me back by the seat of my pants. After I had had several falls, Brown said, "Skate sideways instead of facing the audience." I tried it and it worked, so I gave a perfect performance. Then the manager came back and closed us for cutting out the falls.

Then we got a date to open at the Dewey Theater on Fourteenth Street. In those days managers could close you out after one performance if you didn't go over. Every Monday they booked eight acts and closed four. After our performance we lined up with the other players, backstage, to get the word about who was in and who was out. The manager started down the line, pointed at some acts and said, "You're closed. . . . You're closed. . . . And you're closed." He passed us and said to the acrobatic act next to us, "And you're closed." This was great—we were in! Then the acrobat picked up this little manager by the back of his neck and said, *"Who's* closed?" The manager pointed to us and said, "Brown and Williams."

Now stick with me for a couple of paragraphs, because the going is rough. As I said, after Brown and Williams broke up and we became Brown and Williams, the original Williams joined up with another partner. You now had Brown and Williams and Williams and Brown. Then we split up and they split up. Then you had Brown and Williams, Williams and Brown, Brown and Brown, and Williams and Williams. Then we all split up. Now there were

34

Brown and Williams, Williams and Brown, Brown and Brown, Williams and Williams, the Williams Boys and the Brown Brothers. See what I mean?

Now that you have it clearly in mind who everybody was, here's what happened. Every one of us did exactly the same act: singing, dancing, roller skating. Once, we were all booked into upstate New York at the same time. One act went to Troy, one to Albany, one to Schenectady, one to Mechanicsville, and so on. Our bookings called for us to move from one of these towns to another. When we moved into the second half of that same week, the managers took one look at the same names doing the same acts, and we all came home the same day on the same train. This put such a strain on everybody that the original Brown and Williams went back together and the rest of us sold our skates.

The Williams and Brown episode lasted long enough for me to pay for my gold tooth. Then my mother said, now that I was thirteen and a man, I should settle down and go into a legitimate business. I was able to get a job as a size-ticket boy at a concern called Borgenicht and Kornreich. I printed size tickets for children's dresses from eight in the morning till six at night, Monday through Friday, and until one o'clock on Sunday, and received five dollars a week. This was not much of a salary, so I had to save on transportation costs. I managed this by outwitting the streetcar conductors.

The cars were jam packed at this hour, and the conductor had to work his way through the car to collect the fares. When he got to the front, he jumped

off, and when the back of the streetcar caught up
with him he would jump on and start the routine of
collection all over again. I'd wait for a car that had
a conductor in the middle of it, jump on at the back
and simply follow him, about a half a car behind,
doing exactly what he did, so he never saw me and
I never saw him. All this jumping on and off took
some agility, but it kept me in shape for my dancing,
because it was something like the step "Falling Off
the Log."

I worked for Borgenicht and Kornreich for quite
a while. There were so many people employed there
that we were all given numbers for the purpose of
identification and for punching the time clock. My
number was 78. Mr. Kornreich was always firing
people, but he would only fire you on Friday because
that was the end of the week. If you did something
wrong on Tuesday he would say, "Remind me Friday to fire you." I never did.

I got to be good friends with three other boys
there, because we all sang harmony. There was
Myer Bolomuth, Izzie Mintz, Dave Lefkowitz, and
me. One day the four of us were in the men's room
rendering "My Darling Lulu" when the door opened
and Mr. Kornreich came in. "What's your number?"
he said. I said, "Seventy-eight." "And yours?"
"Sixteen." "And yours?" "Eight." "And yours?"
"Twelve." Kornreich didn't have a pencil so he kept
repeating the numbers to himself as he went out,
"Seventy-eight, sixteen, eight, twelve . . . seventy-
eight, sixteen, eight, twelve . . . seventy-eight, sixteen, eight, twelve." As he walked out of the men's

room, somebody bumped into him. He forgot our numbers and fired four other people.

The loft above Borgenicht and Kornreich was occupied by the Ed Pinaud Company, which made perfume and hair tonic. They employed only girls. The girls broke for lunch at the same time we did, which was perfect for me. I took it upon myself to entertain them with songs, jokes, and dances while they ate. They sat on the steps out in the hall and on the floor above where they could look down through the banisters. This gave me not only a full house but also a gallery. I couldn't have been happier. The audience was large and enthusiastic. Its enthusiasm was not shared, however, by Mr. Kornreich. He came out in the hall one day when I had it packed. At the same time the inspector from the fire department arrived. The inspector fined Kornreich and Kornreich fired me. I should have been more careful; this was a Friday and he didn't even need to be reminded. He also fired Dave Lefkowitz for holding my corned-beef sandwich while I was entertaining.

Before I left Borgenicht and Kornreich, I had been promoted to ply-puller, and then to assistant cutter. Now when you were an assistant cutter, you were on easy street. It was hard work, but the rewards were great. Twelve dollars a week was big money, so when Dave and I were fired, we weren't too upset, particularly Dave, who was a full-fledged cutter and was getting $18 a week. We knew our craft, and figured there was another job around the corner. As it turned out, we were right.

Dave got a job as cutter, and I as assistant cutter

at Mursky and Company, a kimono and wrapper house. These were not what you would call quality garments; they sold for a dollar apiece retail. There were twenty 75-foot tables in the cutting room, and our job was to lay 240 layers of material on one of the tables. The material had to be laid absolutely straight because the straight-knife cutting machine cut right through the pattern on top, all the way down to the lowest level of cloth.

Dave and I were young and cocky and we figured if we worked double speed we could finish twice as fast. We were supposed to finish the allotted work by six, and thought if we finished by noon we could go home and have the rest of the day off. We were never wronger. They just gave us more work. When we found we were doing twice as much work, we asked for twice as much money. We did not get it, so the two of us went on strike against Mursky and Company. We did not break Mursky. There were a thousand employees, and as they went to and from work we were outside picketing. They said hello and we said hello back. This went on for about a week, then we ran out of food and hellos and I looked for another job.

My sisters Mamie and Goldie were working for the Gaiety Waist Company at this time and they were able to get me a job there as a cutter. Their system of cutting was to cut one sleeve, half a front, half a back, half a collar. But you laid the goods face to face and that way you were cutting a whole waist. This was explained to me, and I started to work. Unfortunately my mind, as usual, was on show business. I was entertaining that night at the Red Leaf Circle Club, and I was so busy rehearsing my monologue to myself that before I knew what I was doing, instead of laying the goods face to face I laid it all right side down. I cut 240 dozen half waists that couldn't match.

The next day Mamie, Goldie, and I were all looking for jobs.

At the end of six months of unemployment I was worried because I owed my good friend Dave Lefkowitz thirty-two dollars and felt I must pay him. One job I wouldn't take before was fur cutting. The fur-cutting machines threw off clouds of tiny fine hairs that could cause havoc in the lungs, to say nothing of ruining my singing voice. However, I figured if I worked at it just long enough to repay Dave, it wouldn't hurt me. A short period was what I went after, and a short period is what I got . . . about four days.

I didn't waste my time in those four days. There was a messenger girl named Maxine Jacoby around. During lunch hour I taught her how to dance the Texas Tommy, and by the fourth day I was showing her my whirlwind finish. I had asked her if she would like to go into show business. I'd work with anybody who would work with me. Maxine said she would give me an answer by the end of the week. And as we were talking, I was working a straight-knife machine and cutting through a pile of furs. There was a tack in the table which stopped the machine from moving. I thought the fur was hard to cut or maybe the blade was dull, so I put my foot on the table behind me, I braced myself, and gave a mighty shove. Well, the tack broke, the machine took off and me with it, and we sliced our way through hundreds of dollars' worth of furs.

I arrived on the other end of the table frightened to death. This factory went twenty stories up, and I didn't wait for the elevator. I didn't wait for my salary and I didn't wait for Maxine's answer. And I still owed Dave Lefkowitz thirty-two dollars.

Twelve years later I met Gracie.

The Hot Suit

4

WHEN I was sixteen I wanted everybody to think I had a wonderful personality. I'd be riding all by myself in the subway and I'd sit there and smile. It must have been very noticeable, because I always kept my gold tooth highly polished. I don't know what the other passengers thought, but it never took more than about four stations to have them moving away from me on all sides.

Things had been tough before but never like this period. By this time Mamma had resigned herself to my not becoming a big wheel in the garment industry, and was giving me twenty-five cents a day while I tried to sneak back into show business. I knew that appearance was as important as personality, so I was always dressed to the teeth. I may have been hungry, but my pants were creased. I used to go to a tailor shop at Second Avenue and Fourth Street to get my suit pressed. They charged fifteen cents to press a suit while you stood in back in your underwear. I was always in a hurry and couldn't wait, so I'd put the suit on hot from the steam iron. It took about five blocks to cool off, and I'd walk stiff-legged down the street so as not to wrinkle the pants. I was smoking seven-cent Ricora cigars and wearing pince-nez with a long black ribbon on them. I'd found them, and they must have belonged to a man of seventy. I thought they made me look very distinguished even if they did make me step off of sidewalks that weren't there.

Stiff-legged, with pince-nez, huge cigar, three cents in my pocket, and smiling with my gold tooth shining. . . . Let's face it—nobody knew I was laying off.

One day my mother was shopping and she ran into Mrs. Friedman, a neighbor of ours. Mrs. Friedman said, "Your George is such a nice boy, Mrs. Birnbaum. It's too bad about his legs." "His legs?" said Mamma. "What's the matter with his legs?" "Every morning he passes my house walking stiff-legged and smiling. What a brave boy!" "His legs will be all right," Mamma said. "In fact, he'll be all right." She knew about the hot suit and my wonderful personality. And I *was* all right. I laid off for another six months.

About this time I met two fellers, Hymie Goldberg and Nat Fields. We became very good friends because we were all crazy about show business. Hymie Goldberg worked in a laundry and sang like Belle Baker. Nat Fields was a comedian. We decided to do an act together. By this time I had changed my name to Glide after the finish of one of my favorite dance steps, and Hymie Goldberg

42

changed his to Goldie. We became Goldie, Fields, and Glide, and we entertained at clubs on the East Side.

We used to hang out in front of Katz's umbrella store at Rivington and Clinton streets. One day we were working out a new routine, and Mr. Katz came out and said, "Listen, if you kids want to make some money instead of dancing in the street, I'll make a deal with you. On rainy days, you come here and take a bunch of umbrellas uptown—sell them for a dollar apiece and I'll give you fifty cents for each one you sell." This turned out to be a good deal. The minute it started to rain, we'd each take about fifteen or twenty umbrellas and light out for Broadway where we waited in front of the theaters. Cabs were hard to get, and the umbrellas sold well. During the rainy season Goldie, Fields, and Glide was a successful act. In fact, in one period of inclement weather, we made enough money to have cards and stationery printed and a hundred photographs taken. Goldie, Fields, and Glide had everything— except bookings.

When the weather was good, and things were bad, I used to bring Hymie Goldie home to spend the night. We'd get in about two or three in the morning, always hungry, and always find one egg in the icebox. We'd scramble the egg with lots of milk if there was any, or water if there wasn't. We stretched the egg about as far as it would go and then some.

In the morning Mamma always came out and read the same line. She'd shake her head and say, "I would have sworn there was an egg in the icebox." This was our cue to talk about umbrellas and pretend we didn't hear her. This routine went on for some time.

Then my brother Willie, who was four and slept on a cot in Mamma's room, came to me one day and said, "I'm terribly worried about Mamma. I think she's going crazy." I said, "Why?" He said, "Every once in a while about three o'clock in the morning she laughs so hard the bed shakes." She wasn't crazy —she just heard us frying that egg.

When we finally did get a booking, it was for a Sunday concert at Miner's Bowery. By this time we had the act running pretty smoothly, except for one thing. I told you Hymie used to work in a laundry. Well, he worked there so long that he couldn't sing without moving his arm as if he was ironing. Anyway, we played this Sunday concert. I was the blackface comedian with a wow-wow mouth. I had seen Jolson, and I figured if he was a hit with a big white mouth, I'd be a riot with a bigger one. I had mine on so wide, it went right up behind my ears. In fact, I was pretty nearly a white-face comedian. Nat Fields was the Jewish comedian, and to make sure everyone knew it, he wore a beard and pulled his derby hat down over his ears. Goldie was a tough guy with his hat on sideways. In our last number, I danced, Nat Fields played tissue paper on a comb, and Goldie ironed out two choruses of "My Girl Is a High-Toned Lady." After doing our first show we walked into our dressing room to find the manager, Freeman Bernstein, waiting for us.

"Boys," he said, "I just caught your act, and

44

there's something I want to know." He pointed to Nat Fields who still had on his beard and derby. "What character are you playing?" Nat looked surprised. "Jewish," he answered. "If you're Jewish," said the manager, and he pointed to me as I stood there all blackened up, "then what character are you playing?" He paid us off. That was the end of Goldie, Fields, and Glide. Goldie went back to the laundry and Goldberg. I went back to umbrellas and Burns, and the name Fields I can't do anything with.

At this time, Jack Linder, who later became Mae West's producer, had a booking agency in the Putnam Building. He let me sit in his office, even if there was nothing for me. I figured it looked impressive for me to be sitting there whether there was a job in it or not. One day a booker came in and said, "Do you know where I can find an actor named George Burns?" I jumped to my feet and said, "I'm George Burns." He gave me a contract to play the Myrtle Theater in Brooklyn as a monologist—three days for fifteen dollars. He didn't know I was the wrong George Burns.

I borrowed five dollars more from Dave Lefkowitz and went to Guttenberg's on the Bowery, where I rented a frock coat, gray vest, striped pants, and spats. Thus outfitted, I stole Jim Thornton's act, which didn't fit me—Thornton was a monologist about seventy years old. In those days the performer supplied his own pictures for the front of the theater. If the act didn't go over, the manager simply handed him back his pictures. That meant, "That's all, brother!" It saved them a lot of talking.

45

I Love Her, That's Why!

I opened this day at the Myrtle Theater by walking out on the stage with a rolled-up newspaper under my arm and Jim Thornton's act. The opening line was "Love is like the mumps. The older you are, the harder it goes with you when you get it." I heard someone call and looked into the wings. I said, "Me?" A man nodded yes. I walked off stage. It was the manager. He gave me back my pictures. Although I was closed I still wanted to do a single, so I sold a few more umbrellas and had a song written especially for me which went like this:

> "If you'll notice on the program
> Where it mentions all the turns
> You take a look at number two
> And you see the name of Burns.
> It doesn't say company
> Or anything like that
> It simply says, assisted
> By his little derby hat."

This was the first of six verses. Two months later I was booked into the same Myrtle Theater. As I was rehearsing the act at nine in the morning, the manager came over to me and said, "Are you the Burns of 'Love is like the mumps'?" I said yes. He handed me my pictures again. I guess I'm the first actor who was ever closed before he opened.

A few months later I went in for serious ballroom dancing. I figured if the Castles could be such a hit, with my experience and background I was a cinch. I danced with all kinds of girls—not necessarily pretty ones. I was looking for talent, and if a girl could get on her toes and stay there, I never looked at her face. In the course of searching for the ideal partner, I entered lots of dancing contests and I won a lot of cups. Mamma was proud of them, even though I didn't make enough money to keep her in silver polish. They were always turning black.

Then I started to dance with one girl steady. Her name was Nettie Curlin. She had two recommendations: she was light on her feet, and her father owned a pickle stand. It was hard to beat getting a partner *and* free pickles. We did exhibition dances and were paid five dollars a night.

One night we were dancing at the Stuyvesant Casino. We were doing an eccentric fox trot to a number called "Ragging the Scale." This was danced with all the lights out except a spot which followed us. The dance lasted three or four minutes, and at the end of it a fellow, Jake, who knew me when I was with the Pee Wee Quartette, came up to me and said, "Hey Tootchoo, what do you get for that number?" I said, "Five dollars." He said, "How long does it last?" I said, "About four minutes." He said, "The next time you do it make it ten minutes—and there's an extra twenty-five dollars in it for you." I said, "Are you kidding?" He said, "No. Go down to Freeman's Restaurant on Willett Street in the morning and the money will be waiting." We danced for fifteen minutes. At the end of the dance, they turned the lights up, and Jake and his boys had picked everybody's pocket.

The twenty-five dollars came in very handy. I bought a pair of button shoes with gray suede tops,

47

a gray derby, and a four-button, gray herringbone suit which you only buttoned the top button and kept one hand in the pocket so in case you had any change, you could jangle it. It was not an entirely selfish expenditure of the money, because out of it I also bought Nettie a pair of full-length opera gloves. She was not properly grateful, because the following week, at a dance contest at Tammany Hall on Fourteenth Street, we only came in second. A boy named Georgie Warner won the first prize. He not only won the contest and the cup. He won Nettie too. This was a real blow. I was fond of pickles.

Ten years later, I met Gracie.

My First and Only Blonde

5

LET'S see, how old am I now? I know—seventeen. Well, about this time an agent-producer named Joe Woods who booked kid acts for the small time that were imitations of the Gus Edwards Revues signed me for an act called "The Fourth of July Kids." The act consisted of five boys and four girls ranging in age from fourteen to eighteen.

The boys played characters and danced, the girls sang, danced, and looked pretty. They let me do the singing because I stammered so badly I couldn't read lines. The dialogue didn't match the scenery, and my voice didn't match the arrangements. They were made for a tenor who sang three tones higher than me. I sang "The Red Rose Rag" and "Two Hearts Nestled Closely, Dear, for Quite a While." Trying to reach some of those high notes, I nearly became a toe dancer.

The eldest member of our group was a girl named Mary Murphy. She was eighteen, very tall, and stuck on me. Every time we were in the wings waiting to go on she'd sneak up behind me and give me a little hug. I thought she was pretty fresh, although I could well understand how she found me attractive. I looked great with make-up on and used to put on wonderful lips. I looked quite a lot like Dolores Del Rio.

I considered Mary an old woman. Also when she hugged me too tight, I'd fall off the box I was standing on, but it wasn't that that kept us apart. It was economics. I was making a good salary, fifteen dollars a week. However, I had to send home seven, and at the time I was still smoking Ricora cigars which now cost eight cents apiece. For me to go steady with Mary I would have had to give up the Ricoras. It was a tough decision, but when a man has to make up his mind between a pretty girl and a cigar, there is one obvious choice. I gave her up.

Joe Woods booked the Fourth of July Kids, but another guy whose name I don't remember because I don't want to be sued, owned and managed it. He was awful. We were booked into Gloversville for a three-day trial. The arrangement was that if we were a hit, we would go on to Wilkes-Barre and Scranton. We were not. We thought we were through, but this character told us that we were to wait in Gloversville for word from Woods, who had another booking for us. He told Mary Murphy something else. He was sweet on her but didn't know she was sweet on me. He said he was sneaking out of town, leaving us stranded, but that he would see that she got home. He told her to meet him at the railroad station at two in the morning. She did. But first she told me, and I told the kids, the kids told the cops, and we all met him at the station. We got home, but he stayed in Gloversville for six months.

At the end of this episode I owed Dave Lefkowitz sixty-three dollars.

I was out of show business again, but I never stopped practicing, and was up on my dancing. I was able to get a job at Bennie Bernstein's Dancing School at Second Street and Avenue B. Bernstein couldn't even walk to music, but he was a big success because he spoke seven languages. The immigration laws were wide open and New York was full of newly arrived Poles, Lithuanians, Hungarians, and others who wanted to learn to dance and couldn't speak English. Bernstein would do the talking and I would do the teaching. The admission was ten cents for men, and five cents for ladies. If business was good I was able to make about fifteen dollars a week, and if I could sell a five-dollar-lesson course I could keep a dollar of it. The courses sold better to men. The girls didn't really want to learn to dance; they were just looking to get married.

At the beginning of the evening, all the men would be seated on one side of the hall and the girls on the other. Bernstein would open the dancing by ringing a bell and announcing loudly, "Ladies and gentlemen, when I give the signal, the gentlemen will cross over and ask the ladies to dance—no running, please. And for the last time I'd like to tell you no gentlemen are allowed in the ladies' toilet. . . . Professor Heller's Double Brass Band will now play the mirror dance."

I Love Her, That's Why!

Professor Heller's Double Brass Band consisted of a piano player, drummer, and two trumpets. The Mirror Dance was an invention of Bernstein's. A girl sat in a chair in the middle of the hall with a mirror in her hand. A man crossed the room and looked over her shoulder into the mirror. If she liked his looks, she nodded yes, and got up and danced with him. If not, she nodded no, and the poor dope had to go back to his own side. Between us, no one ever copied this dance.

The two other dancing teachers were girls, and when the men they were teaching were too big or too awkward they turned them over to me. If I say so myself I did a great job. By the end of the course I invariably had the men doing a pretty creditable waltz, fox trot, and two-step. The only trouble was they couldn't do it with anybody but me.

Every night Bernstein made this speech: "Ladies and gentlemen: Please remember that we have dancing in this place Monday night, Tuesday night, Wednesday night, Thursday night, Friday night, Saturday night, Sunday night, and every night in the week." Then once a year he gave a masquerade ball and started to plug it two months in advance. He'd ring his bell and announce: "Ladies and gentlemen: Two months from tonight this dancing school is giving a masquerade ball. It is being held at Hennington Hall. I'll admit that Hennington Hall is not a big hall. Stuyvesant Casino is bigger than Hennington. Hunts Point Palace is bigger than Stuyvesant Casino. Webster Hall is bigger than the Hunts Point Palace. So the answer is: the size of the hall has nothing to do with the ball. Sometimes in a small hall is a big ball. Sometimes in a big hall is a small ball. So you see, the halls have nothing to do with the balls. Now, before the next dance I want to warn you again—gentlemen· are not allowed in the ladies' toilet. Professor Heller will now play 'Sometimes a Smile.' "

One hot summer night, business was terrible; there were about eighteen people in the room. It looked more like the funeral of a very unpopular fellow than a group of people out to enjoy themselves. Bernstein got a brilliant idea. He moved the band over under the windows which opened onto the street. He figured if they played out to the street instead of into the hall, the people outside would hear the music and come in. It was a fine idea. What happened was, the people outside, hearing the music, started to dance in the street. In no time it was a block party, and our eighteen customers joined them.

Well, after a while business picked up. I was making about twenty-five a week, and Bernstein asked me to be his partner. We opened B.B.'s (Bernstein and Burns, that is) College of Dancing on Pitkin Avenue in Brownsville, Brooklyn. A guy came in one night and checked a package before he went in to dance. A couple of hours later the police arrived, arrested him, and in looking around found the package in the checkroom. They took the man, Bernstein, and· me to the police station. It seems this man hit a woman over the head in a Broadway hotel and robbed her. The package contained her money and jewels. They let Bernstein and me go, but a few weeks later they closed our place because they said it was "a breeding place for lounge lizards." And that was the end of the B.B. College of Dancing, but I never regretted it because at the Pitkin Avenue place I met my one and only blonde.

Her name was Gertha LaMotte. What a thrill I got the first time I danced with her! It had been so long since I danced with a girl. Anyway, I was so mad about her I finally decided to take her home to mother. We walked in the door and I said, "Mamma, I want you to meet my sweetheart." Mamma took in everything. Now in those days, if a girl wore a little rouge on her cheeks she was no better than a ——. Gertha not only wore rouge. She had beaded eyelashes. Mamma smiled and said, *"Gay in d'rerd,"* which means "Go to hell" in Yiddish. Then she turned to Gertha and said, "I just told my son what a wonderful girl you are."

Mamma being Mamma, the subject of Gertha didn't come up again until a few weeks later. I had a date with her. I was getting dressed and couldn't find a clean collar, so I put on one of my oldest brother Morris's. I had a size-thirteen neck and his was a seventeen, so my head kept disappearing. Mamma came in and said, "Where are you going with that collar? You look ridiculous. I'll wash and iron one of yours and it will dry under the iron." As she was ironing she said, "Who are you going out with tonight?" "Gertha LaMotte," I answered. She stopped and said, "Wear Morris's collar."

Nine years later I met Gracie.

Big Rose Cohen and Little Rose Cohen

6

FOR the next two years I never knew what my name was. After playing a theater I would have to change my name. The booker who booked me would never give me another job if he knew who I was. It never crossed my mind that there was any reason to change the act, so I changed my name instead. I changed my name so many times that I got so I answered to anything. If I walked down the street and someone said, "Hello, Newman," I'd say "Hello." Who knew?—it might be me. I played Red Bank, New Jersey, one week under the name of Jimmy Delight and the next week as Billy Pierce. In fact, I played Red Bank so many times that one day when the manager was at the station when my train pulled in, he wouldn't even let me get off the train.

Even though the jobs were few and far between, I always put a little makeup on the edge of my collar so that everybody would think I was working. Then I thought it was time to try a double again and I teamed up with a girl named Janie Malone. I decided Jed Jackson was a good name for me that week, and we became Jackson and Malone. We were booked into the Grand Opera House on Twenty-third Street. The act started with a single by me, a song called "If You're Crazy About the Women, You're Not Crazy at All." Then Janie came out and we did a dance number, then she went off and I did some syncopated patter against music, followed by a buck dance with little cymbals in my heels. Then we both put on wooden shoes and did a double buck.

The manager, who had seen us billed as a double out front, came into the theater just as I came on for my opening song. He watched for a couple of minutes, then said, "That's funny—this act is supposed to be a double act." He started for backstage, which in this theater meant going outdoors and around to the back of the theater. By the time he got there, Janie and I had done our dance and I was on alone again doing my patter. He went into the dressing room to wait for me, and Janie came on again for the finish. He never did see her. I walked into the dressing room and he said, "Look, Jackson, isn't this supposed to be a double act?" I said, "That's right." He said, "And somebody was working with you on the stage just now?" "That's right." He gave me a strange look and said, "Well, let me tell you something. I've been manager here seventeen years and you're the first single double act that's ever played my theater." I don't know what report he sent in to the booking agent, but that week Janie went back to running an elevator and I became Jimmy Ferguson.

Big Rose Cohen and Little Rose Cohen

A little while later, I joined up with another guy, and we called the act Burns and Links. My name was Links. Confusing, isn't it? We did a two-man dancing act, and couldn't get a job anywhere. We were sitting outside Farley Marcus's office one day. Marcus was a small-time booking agent for one-nighters. He had a swinging door which opened into his inner office through which we could hear snatches of conversation. On one swing, we heard him say, "I could use a dog act in Ronkonkoma." I went to his secretary and said, "Tell Mr. Marcus that Burns and Links and their dogs are sitting outside." She went in and told him. He gave us a contract to play Ronkonkoma one night for ten dollars. We went to Forty-fourth Street, picked up two dogs, and went to fulfill the engagement. The act opened with eight bars of an introduction, "Down Among the Sheltering Pines," pianissimo, offstage, then a repeat of eight bars same, forté, and we would run onstage holding our straw hats high in the air with one hand so the audience could see the red linings. This time we ran out, hats in the air, and dogs under our arms. We dropped the dogs, finished the act, collected the ten dollars, and I changed my name again.

I finally ran out of names and bookings and went back to Burns and ballroom dancing. The success of the Castles had stimulated all the ballrooms into holding contests with big-money prizes to develop young talent. My talent didn't need developing, but my cash balance did, so I entered every contest around, and after five or six, was able to finally pay off Dave Lefkowitz. The tango was the dance of the day, and I went for it in a big way. My sideburns were the talk of Second Avenue. The other popular dance was the Peabody, which was originated by a Captain Peabody of the New York Police Force. He was a truly great dancer who could have been one of the greatest of all time if he hadn't preferred being a cop. Some of the steps he originated are still being used by dance teams today. I was one up on the other contestants because I had two steady partners, Big Rose Cohen and Little Rose Cohen. Big Rose Cohen was a wonderful tango dancer, and Little Rose Cohen did a terrific Peabody. I was pretty well fixed to win a contest with either one or the other of them.

One night, one of the year's biggest contests was being held at Jardin de Dance, which later became Loew's Roof. It was an interborough affair with all five boroughs competing. The first prize was $250. They didn't announce ahead of time what the prize dance was to be, but I was prepared: I took *both* Rose Cohens with me. Tango or Peabody, I was out to win. Then, after a roll of drums, the announcer cried, "Ladies and gentlemen: The dance the contest will be judged by is an eccentric fox trot!" Well, don't think for a minute this cramped my style. I went over to Georgie Warner, who was there with Nettie Curlin, borrowed Nettie, won the first prize, split it five ways, and Georgie, Nettie, I, and the two Rose Cohens left with fifty dollars apiece.

One night a few weeks later, I was doing an exhibition dance at P.S. 188. After my performance, when everybody danced, I noticed one girl in particular; she was really good. I didn't hesitate to ask for an introduction. I figured I was more or less doing her a favor. She couldn't help but be impressed by me. I had had a look in the mirror in the hall and was pretty impressed with myself. I was not only the celebrity of the evening but a smart dresser—blue suit, black-and-white-checked vest, bell-bottomed trousers, and my sideburns ran right down into my collar. What more could you want? I got Marcy Klauber to introduce us. Her name was Hannah Siegal and we clicked right away. She was a good all-around dancer—Peabody, tango, fox trot—so I asked her to team up with me. We worked out an act, and this time I changed her name instead of mine. I chose Hermosa José. She thought it was a beautiful name and that I was original and clever to have thought of it. She didn't know I was smoking José Hermosa cigars.

After we won all the dance contests around, we went into vaudeville and didn't do too badly. We opened with a Spanish number. She wore a bright-red dress covered with rhinestones. It had only one sleeve. With it she wore long earrings and a Spanish comb. I wore a "walk up a flight and save $10" full-dress suit that was supposed to be black but after one cleaning turned green. It also shrank so much with each successive cleaning that the elastic loop on the bottom of the vest, which was there to button to the top of the pants to hold the vest down, now was pulling the pants up. With this I wore a flat Valentino hat with a cord under the chin.

As the curtains parted, we were found stage center, she with one hand over her head and one hand on her hip, and left foot pointed, and me with my hands behind my back, right foot pointed. As the music started I took off my hat and threw it into the wings, which I always missed. Now just to show you we knew what time it was, we were both dressed in Spanish clothes and dancing to a piece of music called "La Czarina," which was a Russian mazurka.

The act played in and around New York for a while, but never more than a week anywhere. Then we got a call from a booking agent who offered us thirty-six weeks on the road. We were supposed to leave on a Monday, but Thursday of the week before, Hermosa's parents decided they wouldn't let her go on the road with me unless we were married. We certainly weren't going to cancel thirty-six weeks, so we were married. We played the thirty-six weeks, and returned to New York where we faced the fact that what we were both in love with was show business, not each other. So we broke up the act and the marriage.

My brother Isadore H. (the original George) was now running a successful women's clothing store in Akron, Ohio. He wanted me to quit show business and come out and work for him, because he didn't think I was getting anywhere. I can't think why, I'd been in this line of work for thirteen years and I had four beautiful pairs of spats. Isadore was worried about my lack of education. He didn't think four years were enough. So he said if I would go to a preparatory school for a year, he'd have a job waiting for me when I got out. I went for two weeks. I tried to pay attention, but I didn't get much of what my teacher was saying because my mind was on trying to switch a few gags from *College Humor*.

Big Rose Cohen and Little Rose Cohen

Maybe I should have listened because my teacher, Leon Trotsky, made quite a splash later. For the record, I never stole any of his material.

This was the era of the speak-easy, and a bunch of us used to go to a joint in Chinatown called Sirrocco's. It was sort of Bronx–Moorish in design, and the lookout outside carried a gun under his burnoose. There was a girl named Gypsy who worked there. I danced with her a few times and I thought she liked me, but I wasn't sure until my friend Bucky Hamel said one night, "You know, Gypsy is crazy about you. In fact, she asked me why I didn't bring you down here more often." This went straight to my head. Gypsy was an older woman and very exotic. It got so that Bucky and I went to Sirrocco's two or three times a week. I'd dance all evening with Gypsy. I thought Bucky was quite a pal. He'd sit alone and he would buy me a beer—the big glass—while I danced the evening away. And a few times he'd take me to dinner. It was always chop suey. He'd serve it. He took the chop suey and I got the noodles. But I didn't mind; it was his forty cents. And besides, I love noodles. They make a noise when you eat them.

Then one night a waiter tipped me off. It seems Gypsy was so crazy about my dancing that she made a deal with Bucky to give him five dollars every time he brought me in. He was getting fifteen dollars a week, and I was finishing up with those noisy noodles. My disillusion was complete. I gave up Bucky and Gypsy and haven't looked at a noodle since.

Seven years later I met Gracie.

61

No Talent, but Nice Vests

7

WHEN I was twenty-four I became a quiet dresser. I started by cutting off my sideburns—the tango was going out anyway; then I replaced my gold tooth, and finally took the white piping off the top of my vest.

I took on this conservative appearance and a new act simultaneously. I joined with two girls named the Rosebud Sisters in a singing and dancing act. These girls always wore long dresses, even though short ones were in style at the time. One of them was terribly bowlegged and the other dressed that way to match her. When they did high kicks, they always turned sideways to the audience.

About this time I started to eat in a restaurant called Wiennig and Sberber's on Forty-fifth Street. Maybe I'd better tell you something about Wiennig and Sberber's. It was quite a place. It was a hangout for actors, song writers, prize fighters, and correspondents. To give you an idea of what Sberber's character was, he was the kind of man who smelt everything before he bought it. This habit started with cigars, but it expanded into everything else. If a man came in to sell him napkins, for instance, he'd put one to his nose, sniff it, and say, "I'll take a dozen." This went for chairs, crockery, and everything else he purchased. He also got into every conversation, spoke with authority on every subject, and never knew what he was talking about.

One night I was just starting dinner, and had started on the pile of bread in the middle of the table that was so high you couldn't see anyone across the table from you. I was humming to myself, and Sberber came over to the table and said, "Burns, the way you are singing, I can tell you like music." I said, "Why? Do you like music?" He said, "Do I like music? I come from Chicago." I said, "Is that so? You're a lover of music?" "Music," he said. "My daughter even took singing lessons." Knowing Sberber, I said, "By any chance did she take lessons from a man named La Guardia? I wonder if you know him?" "Know him!" said Sberber. "He charges fifteen dollars a lesson." I said, "Do you like good music?" "Do I like good music?" he said. "I'm always at the opera; I've seen *La Bohème* maybe sixteen, seventeen times. I know it by heart." "Is that so?" I said. "How does it go?" He said, "Good."

Well, that will give you an idea about Sberber. Wiennig was a different type of character. He was the kind who only remembered his last conversation. If you asked him a question he gave you the answer to the last customer's question. It went something like this: I walked in one day and said, "Hello, Mr.

I Love Her, That's Why!

Wiennig. Have you seen Manny Mannishaw?" He said, "Look on the floor, maybe it fell down there." He never called the customers by their names but by the act they had made famous at the moment. Jolson would come in and Wiennig would say, "Give April Showers the second table." And he'd greet Eddie Leonard with, "How's Rolly Boly Eyes today?" That was Wiennig.

Just to round things out, the waiters also were characters. They were terribly busy, and wasted no time with small talk. One day a customer came in and said, "Where's the men's room?" and a waiter said, "Please—I've only got two hands!" None of the waiters trusted each other, because they stole one another's tips, so when they had to go for an order they backed into the kitchen and yelled, "One roast beef!" without turning their heads.

The phone was on the wall. To answer it, you had to turn your back to the customers. When it rang, and Wiennig or Sberber went to answer it, all the customers picked up lumps of sugar. The proprietors would grab the receiver off the hook while they looked at the customers. Then they'd turn back in to the phone, holler "Hello" and duck, and all the customers threw the lumps of sugar at them. This was a running gag and one of their main attractions. One day they got sick of this bit, changed to granulated sugar; but business fell off so they went back to lumps again. Well, that gives you a picture of Wiennig and Sberber on Forty-fifth Street.

I was having breakfast there one morning before going to rehearse the music for my act with the

Rosebud sisters, and a feller came in and offered to sell me some scenery for ten dollars. In those days, if you carried your own scenery you automatically received twenty-five dollars more a week. This seemed like a good deal, so I bought it and told him I'd pay him if and when I got paid. We were booked into Fox's City Theater on Fourteenth Street. I had the scenery on my shoulder, tried to get on either a subway or trolley, and they refused me, so I walked from Forty-fifth to Thirteenth. When I arrived, panting, the rehearsal was over. I went to the basement to talk over my act with the orchestra leader.

I never did see the scenery, but the feller who sold it to me said it had a center entrance. So I told the Rosebud sisters: "To make this look like it was made for us, one of you girls come out from one side of the stage, one of you from the other, and I'll make my entrance through the center." Our opening was a very jazzy arrangement of "Balling the Jack." As we went into the number, they turned out all the lights, and the manager pulled us from the stage. The scenery that feller had sold me was the interior of a church. That was the end of the Rosebud sisters. They left me; I left the scenery. If anyone has an act that would fit that piece of scenery, they have my permission to use it.

At this time I was living in the apartment of a friend, Mike Marx. He was very nice to me and let me use the place, and if I say so myself, I kept the apartment very clean. I always was a good housekeeper. Once or twice a week instead of sleeping at Mike Marx's, I'd go home. Mamma had moved to

Brooklyn and as usual, when she moved, several of my sisters and brothers-in-law and their families moved into the same apartment building. It wasn't so much that my sisters couldn't bear to be away from her, but that all my brothers-in-law were in love with her. One night I arrived and Mamma was listening to both sides of an argument between my sister Mamie and her husband Max. When she had heard them out, she told my sister she was wrong. "Your husband is right," she said. "Go home, and never bring it up again." They went away, and later she sent me out to the drugstore to call Max and tell him to come over alone. When he arrived, she said, "Max, Mamie was right, and you were wrong, but she'll never hear it from me." And she never did. No wonder they were all in love with her.

After the Rosebud sisters I laid off long enough to run up a bill at Wiennig's of $163, at 35 cents a meal. Then I joined a feller named Sid Garry in a typical small-time Number Two act. We stayed together about two years. We played the Western vaudeville circuit and the Loew's circuit. One week we played Loew's Providence. As we were dressing to go on, I said to Sid, "We ought to call this act 'Two Boys from Rhode Island in an Act of Providence.'" He never answered me.

We were in this theater when we got a phone call from an agent who said he could book us into Keith's Theater in Boston to replace a dancing act in a Sunday concert. In Boston they didn't allow dancing on Sunday. We were a singing-and-talking act. Keith's was real big time and I okayed the date immediately.

He said, "Not so fast. I'll call you by twelve tonight to confirm it." We knew that meant he was trying to get somebody else. He was stuck with us. At twelve an angry voice said, "Be in Boston at ten for a music rehearsal," and hung up on me. We stayed up half the night cleaning our stage suits with benzene. They were brown suits with four-button vests, two of which we cut off to give them a tuxedo effect. With them we wore brown derbies, brown ties, and light-brown spats. We were ready for the big time.

Our act opened with me coming out on the stage and saying, "Has anyone seen a beautiful girl with a beautiful singing voice?" This was Sid Garry's cue to sing offstage in a high soprano voice, "Give Me All of You, Dear, or Give Me None." Then Garry would walk out onstage, still singing, and the audience would see it was a man and that was always good for a big laugh. This was a good opening, but it wasn't ours. We stole it from Milo, a tramp comedian. Well, this Sunday at Keith's, at rehearsal in the morning, the Klein Brothers, who were on the same bill, came over to us and said, "Are you fellers doing that joke about 'Is there a woman in the house I didn't kiss?' " We said yes. He said, "That's our joke." The big brother hit me in the nose. The little one hit Garry. We got the benzene out again and eliminated the joke.

At that matinee, I went into the act with the usual "Anyone see a beautiful girl with a beautiful voice?" And Garry, instead of singing soprano, sang the off-stage song in baritone, which didn't help our open-

67

ing. We struggled through the performance, and when we were in our dressing room I said to Garry, "Why didn't you sing soprano? What happened?" Garry said, "I saw Milo in the front row and I didn't want to get punched in the nose again." Those days, if the managers liked you they sent in a manager's report, and you were called back. This Keith's manager's report said, "Burns and Garry: no talent but nice vests."

Another funny thing that happened to Garry and myself—or rather, *now* it's funny—was at the Folly Theater in Brooklyn. This theater had a sort of horseshoe stage which curved out into the audience, so that the boxes were behind the actors. If you happened to step out of the box you were in back of the actors. This was nervous-making for the actors, because, believe me, this was a tough and hep audience. In our act, Sid Garry did a song that had an eight-bar yodeling finish. He yodeled beautifully, and no matter what song we switched to, he'd add this finish; even if it didn't fit, he loved it.

This particular night, he was singing, "Wouldn't It Be a Wonderful Summer If the Boys Were All Back Home?" Before he got to the last eight bars he went into the yodel of "Go to Sleep, My Baby, My Baby," and when he got to the last baby, and as he fooled around with the top note, we had a dramatic effect: we had a baby spot on him which got smaller and smaller and smaller until it only covered his face. As he hit his top note, a fist came into this baby spot and hit him. Needless to say, we got out the benzene again. I hate to brag, but I would say we

68

used benzene in about three or four hundred theaters.

Our headliner that week was an act named Jim Gibson and Company. Gibson was about fifty and his act consisted of a lot of kids between sixteen and nineteen, and they were a riot. He did a great selling job, and he took about ten or fifteen curtain calls. Gibson came on the stage, walked to the center, looked at the audience and said, "Ladies and gentlemen: You've been a wonderful audience. Thank you so much on behalf of myself and the kids. Now to show my appreciation, how would you like to hear my wife sing a song?" A man in the ninth row said, "I wouldn't." Gibson, stunned, said, *"What?"* The man said, "Look, Mr. Gibson, I loved your act; it's great; I applauded my hands off. But you played here before and I heard your wife sing. You asked me a question, and I answered it." Gibson never used that closing line again, and his wife is still standing in the wings with make-up on.

After this we played the Loew's circuit. We were playing Oklahoma City, and I came out the stage door one night and there was a sad-looking guy sitting in a green Marmon car. He was crying. I couldn't imagine a guy with a Marmon car crying, so I went over to him and said, "What's the matter? Anything I can do for you?" He snuffled and said, "I just had a fight with my girl, and ten minutes ago, I saw her go into a restaurant with my best friend. I've got all the money in the world, and enough oil wells, too, so I'll never have to worry, and I'm miserable. I guess you just can't buy love."

I Love Her, That's Why!

I said, "Oh, maybe it's not as bad as it seems. Have you tried making her jealous? Going out with somebody else yourself?"

"It might work," he said, "if I knew somebody she doesn't know."

"Well," I said, "now maybe I came along at just the right moment. We have an act on the bill with us called 'Sweet Sweeties.' One of the girls is very pretty. I'll introduce you to her now. You can take her to the same restaurant, and maybe it will make your girl jealous and you can get her back."

He said, "Why are you doing all this for me?" I said, "I never rode in a green Marmon car. Let me know if the strategy works." And it did. He took the Sweet Sweetie out. His girl got jealous. He got her back. I got a ride.

That week we became fast friends. His name was Walter McCann, and he was so grateful to me for straightening out his affairs that he introduced me to a beautiful Indian girl named Gladys Trueblood who lived in the same hotel he and I and most of our company did. And *Gladys* and I became fast friends.

One night she asked me to her room to listen to some records—yeah, records, that is. I dressed for the occasion in my pongee kimono that I had bought in Vancouver. The sleeves were so long that on my way down to her room I had to hold my hands up in the air to keep from stepping on them. I was sitting in her room, listening to these records, of course, and to make sure we didn't disturb the other guests we stuffed some towels into the horn of the phonograph. About one o'clock, there was a knock at the door. It was the house detective. There was I, Nathan Birnbaum, in a Japanese kimono, with an Indian girl, listening to John McCormack sing "When Irish Eyes Are Smiling." I knew I was in trouble, and the detective knew it, too. He tried to shake me down for $100—$100 or jail, the terms were. I had six. I offered him that and the kimono. No deal. I couldn't get to first base. It looked as if he was going to take me in. I pleaded with him and he gave me thirty minutes to get the money.

I hated to leave him alone with Gladys Trueblood. He didn't seem to be a music lover. But I had no choice. I went to Sid Garry and told him my problem. He had ten dollars. I took it, and then went up to Walter McCann's suite. I knew he'd have the money, and thought he would help me. After I told him the story he said, "Don't worry about a thing. I'll go down and straighten it out." And he did. He went down to Gladys' room with me and fired the house detective. He owned the hotel. Walter and I stayed in Gladys' room until two-thirty, and being in the company of the owner, we played the phonograph with the towels out of the horn.

The rest of the time I was on the road, I corresponded with Gladys Trueblood. Then we arrived back in New York and I went straight home. It was one o'clock in the morning. As I came in, Mamma said, "Wake up, everybody. Turn on the lights. Nat's home." As soon as she could see me, she said, "How much money did you make?" I said, "Well, I didn't make any, but—" She said, "Turn out the lights, you can tell me in the morning."

I Love Her, That's Why!

A few days later, as I was reading a postcard from Gladys, Mamma said, "Look, Nat, you should break this up. If you want to be a Catholic, that's one thing; but I just can't see you as an Indian." I sold my feathers.

Three years later, I met Gracie.

The Yankee Doodle Blues

8

AFTER a year or so on the road with Garry, we split up and I returned to New York and Wiennig's. Both were unchanged. New York was cold, busy, and unaware that I'd been away; Wiennig's was warm, busy, and glad to see me. The waiters' personalities were also unchanged. They were still rushing.

Although I didn't come out with a profit from the Burns and Garry period, I had made enough to clear up my account with Wiennig. I paid him the $163 and, with full stomach and re-established credit, I started throwing lumps of sugar at Wiennig again when he phoned, and looked around for a new partner. I had learned a lot on the road, and the experience was valuable to me. I had given bad performances in theaters in pretty nearly every Eastern state, but this had been my first opportunity to be bad out West. Now I'd used up every name and every state, and was back to keeping house for Mike Marx, and looking for a new act.

I Love Her, That's Why!

One night I heard a man named Billy Lorraine sing. I liked him and asked him if he'd like to join up with me. He said no but he meant yes. You see, he stuttered, and didn't want anyone to know it, so he always said the word that came out with the least trouble. At the moment, no was easier than yes. So we joined up. We called our act "Burns and Lorraine —Two Broadway Thieves." This was because we imitated Broadway stars neither one of us had ever seen. Billy did Jolson, Eddie Leonard, and Eddie Cantor. I did George White and George M. Cohan. We opened with a double song, then syncopated patter, and then our imitations. Billy was a nice boy and a wonderful performer. The only thing that held him back was his stammer. He was like a lot of people who had this affliction, in that he was all right when he sang, or when he talked in syncopation.

Once we were booked into Pittsburgh and Billy was supposed to pick up our railroad tickets. There was a pretty girl in the ticket office, and Billy liked pretty girls. They also liked him. He took one look at this one. She said, "Where do you want to go?" He tried to say "Pittsburgh," and bought two tickets to Philadelphia.

Another time, we were playing Buffalo. We were in a hotel lobby, and talking about Billy's problem. I said, "Billy, your trouble is you don't open your mouth. If you don't open your mouth the words won't come out. It's like they're in prison—you don't relax. Now let's try something. Your room is on the fifth floor. Get into that elevator and say 'Five.' But before you go," I said, "let me hear you say 'Five.'"

74

He said, "Five."
I said, "Again."
He said, "Five."
I said, "Again."
He said, "Five."
"Once more."
"Five."
"Now," I said, "go to the back of the elevator and just say 'Five.' "

Billy got in the elevator, and when they got to the twenty-second floor the elevator girl said "All out," and Billy walked down seventeen flights.

Now when there was no pressure on Billy he didn't stammer at all.

Once, between trains at five o'clock in the morning, Billy said, "While we wait for the train let's get some ham and eggs." As we walked into the coffee shop Billy said, "Ham and eggs never sounded so good." The waitress was a very pretty girl. She said to me, "What will you have?" I said, "Ham and eggs." She said to Billy, "What'll you have?" He wanted ham and eggs, but he just stared at the girl and said, "I-I-I-I'll t-t-take an oyster omelette."

Billy and I had tough sledding, and any job was a good job. Our agents, Rose and Curtis, had an offer for us for three days into Proctor's Newark for $62.50. I generally handled the business for the act, but they couldn't find me, so they got Billy on the phone. Jack Curtis said, "Would you and Burns like to go to Proctor's Theater Monday, Tuesday, and Wesdnesday for sixty-two fifty?" Billy stood at the phone for five minutes trying to get out an answer, shook his head "yes," and hung up. They got another act.

Then we were booked on the Pantages circuit. This was thirty-four weeks altogether. You played seventeen weeks getting to the Coast, then, in San Francisco, Alexander Pantages looked at the act. If he liked it you got the other seventeen weeks going back. We were in Portland, on our way to the Coast, and Billy had a little trouble for the first time with the words in one of our songs. The song went this way:

BILLY: "I'll take her around the world to spend our honeymoon."

ME: "I never knew the world was in a furnished room."

BILLY: "All she'll get is the best."

ME: "Yes, the sleeves off your vest."

BILLY: "Oh, no."

ME: "Oh, yes."

Then we went into our soft-shoe dance. Well, this afternoon in Portland he got to the line, "I'll take her around the world to spend our honeymoon," and on the word "moon" he started to stutter. In the dressing room I said, "Billy, it's all right to stutter on the word 'moon' in Portland, but next week we play San Francisco, and Pantages will be out front. If you stutter on that word next week, we'll jump from San Francisco to New York, and on our salaries that's quite a jump."

He said, "A-a-a-don't worry, I won't stutter on the word 'moon.' "

The next Monday we walked out on the stage of

the Pantages Theater in San Francisco and went into our song. Mr. Pantages, as usual, was out front. We were doing fine, then Billy got to that line and he sang, "I'll take her around the world to spend our honeym-m-m—" and I didn't wait. I sang, "I never knew the world was in a furnished room." He sang, "All she'll get is the best." I sang, "Yes, the sleeves off your vest." He sang, "Oh, no." I sang, "Oh, yes," and Billy sang, "Moon." He finally made it. It didn't hurt us any. They took up our option for the other seventeen weeks.

From there we went to Los Angeles and were living at the Continental Hotel. Monday morning at the theater, as usual, I was upstairs rehearsing our music and Billy was downstairs in the dressing room unpacking our trunks. Billy rushed up suddenly, white as a sheet. He couldn't get out what he was trying to say, and he tried until I couldn't stand it any longer and said, "Billy—*sing* it!"

He sang, "We were just robbed!"

Well, after we replaced our costumes that had been stolen we started back on the road. There was a girl on the bill with us, doing a single, named Dolly Kraeger. She liked me, and I liked her because she laughed at my jokes. We started going together and had a fine time. She was good company and a good dancer. She never told me that she was keeping steady company with a gangster in Detroit. When we played Seattle, she got a letter from him that said, "I hear you're going with an actor. If this is true I'm coming out to kill him. And just to prove to you that I've got the guts to do it, after I mail this letter I'm going to shoot myself in the leg." And he did. This boy wasn't bright. For the next two months he was limping while Dolly and I were dancing. However, when the tour got within shooting distance of Detroit, I detoured, and she married him. It was better that way. By that time she knew all my jokes.

After we finished the Pantages circuit we were booked into Philadelphia. I was staying at the Hurley House where I had a room with a bathroom in between my room and next door which I shared with a man I had never seen, probably a traveling salesman. I was sitting in my room one night after the show, minding my own business and writing a letter home, when there was a quick knock on the bathroom door. I unlocked it, and this man threw a girl into my room and told me to lock the door again. So I did. What had happened was, this man had the girl in his room and Mr. Hurley found out about it and came up to investigate. So when Mr. Hurley knocked on his door the man got rid of her.

After Hurley left, the man opened the door and wanted his girl back. But she had caught our act at the Paramount Theater and thought I was kind of nice and she wouldn't leave. You can't blame a girl for wanting to better herself. The man went back to his room, called Hurley, and told him he'd got the wrong feller, it was the man next door who had a girl in his room. Hurley rushed up and knocked on my door. I threw the girl back. Then *I* called Hurley . . . then *he* called Hurley . . . then *I* called Hurley . . . well, anyway, after about seven calls, the girl got tired and went home and the man and I went out to dinner.

After Philadelphia we were booked into New York where we played the Moss and Brill time. The bookers wanted to see our act again, on the basis that if they liked the improvements we had made they would raise our pay, which would bring our Eastern salary up to $175 a week. We opened at the Broadway Theater at Broadway and Forty-first Street. In those days, they gave out numbered rehearsal checks: one, two, three, etc. Whoever got to the theater first got the low numbers. I stayed up all night to get rehearsal check number one, because I had heard that Sybil Vane, the headliner on the show, was doing the same song we were. The rule was that in case of duplication of material, the first to rehearse it got to do it. Having squatters' rights, we were allowed to do the song, but the booker of the theater asked us to drop it in favor of the headliner. I said, "Nothing doing! It's a riot for us, and our twenty-five-dollar raise depends on it!" So we did it. It was called "Yankee Doodle Blues." The finish of the song went like this: "Make me lose those Yankee Doodle, I don't want 'em, you can have 'em, Yankee Doodle blues."

We finished the song, each with our left foot over the footlights, our right hands extended with our hats in them, waiting for applause. Two fellers in the front row reached up and took our hats. We laid an egg, we lost the hats, Sybil Vane got the song back, and we didn't get the raise.

While I was working with Billy, I never was far

from Wiennig's. There were a couple of sisters who. used to eat there too; their names were Beverly and Lila Mitchell, and Billy and I and the girls became great friends—just friends. They liked to dance and. so did we. If they were ever in a spot, we'd.help them, and they'd do the same for us.

Once, the phone waked me at two o'clock in the; morning. It was Lila. "George," she said, "Beverly and I are in trouble. We're at the Kit Kat Klub on Forty-fourth Street. We're with a couple of guys who want us to go up to their apartment. Can you come down quickly and pretend you're our brother? You've got to get us out of this."

I did. I made an anxious-brother entrance, said,. "Come on, girls, it's late. We'll hop in a cab and go home." Well, I read this line beautifully, but it had. the most surprising effect. These fellows knew me,. and knew the girls weren't my sisters. But I didn't. know they knew it. They were *very* polite.

One of them said, "You must let us drive you—my car is right outside." I protested. They insisted. I was really in a spot. I had to let them drive us somewhere. We got in the car and one of them said, "Where to?" I said, "Where to? About twenty miles —Brooklyn, Eastern Parkway. My mother's waiting up for us." I was smart. I knew they wouldn't drive us that far.

Anyway, when we arrived at Eastern Parkway we all got out of the car and they walked right up to the door of the apartment with us. So what could I do? I knocked on the door, Mamma opened the door and in we went—Lila, Beverly, and I. Mamma moved the family around a little. Lila slept with Theresa and Goldie; Beverly with Sadie and Mamie, and I was back in bed again with Willie and Sammy.

In the morning we told the family the whole story; which they thought was very funny. You may not, but it stays in anyway. Simon and Schuster ordered eighty thousand words in this book and they're going to get them.

All the time I was working with Billy Lorraine, I was developing material for a new act of my own. I had been noticing that most of the girls in the chorus were just as good dancers as I was, and I figured that if this was the case I'd better work out something else to do if I wanted to stay in show business. I decided on a talking act, a comedy, for two people. I read all the jokes in the magazines and switched the jokes around, and my idea of switching was, if I got it out of *Whiz Bang* I said it came from *College Humor*. My pockets were so loaded with these switches that all I could fasten was the top button of my four-button pin-stripe. In fact, the bottom of the coat was so wide-spread I always looked as if I was making an entrance.

The last date Billy Lorraine and I played was at the Union Hill Theater in New Jersey. There was an act on the bill called Rena Arnold and Company. Rena was the headliner. She was on next to closing —that means next to the last on the bill. I told you that before, but the reason I'm telling you again is that later on an anecdote depends upon it. After the matinee I was talking to Rena Arnold and I told her that Billy and I were splitting up and that I was going to do a talking act. I figured that as long as we were in a conversation anyway, I'd pick up a laugh by telling her a little joke. It was the one about my brother and the pineapples. It was slightly risqué. She didn't enjoy it, and the reason I'm not telling you is you wouldn't either.

That same day, a friend of Rena's came backstage to see her. She was a pretty little Irish girl with long shiny black hair and green eyes. Rena said to her, "You're looking to work with someone. Burns and Lorraine are splitting. Why don't you talk to them? Or rather, why don't you talk to Lorraine. I just talked to Burns and I wouldn't recommend your working with him; he's not very nice. In fact, he's *terrible!*"

The girl went out front to watch our act, came back afterward, and went up to Billy Lorraine and introduced herself. She said, "I'm a friend of Rena Arnold's. I understand you're looking for a new partner, and I am, too. You are Mr. Lorraine, aren't you?" Billy was staring at her—she was *so* pretty. He said, "A-a-no. My name is Burns." She said, "Excuse me," and backed hurriedly away.

She came over to me.

"Miss Arnold said you were looking for a partner," she said.

"I am," I said. "Why don't you meet me at the restaurant in front of the Palace at twelve tomorrow? We'll have breakfast and talk it over. Maybe we can work out something."

"All right," she said. "Good-by, Mr. Lorraine."

82

We had breakfast and talked over the act, and it was very pleasant. She certainly was pretty.

One hour later, I paid my check, she paid her check, and we made a rehearsal date.

Two days later we started to rehearse.

Three days later I told her to stop calling me Lorraine, my name was Burns.

Two years later *her* name was Burns.

By the way—that was Gracie.

9

GRACIE and I didn't have much trouble deciding on an act. She had one she wanted to do. I had one I wanted to do. Her act called for a piece of scenery that would have cost $250. I didn't have two dollars and fifty cents. Mine was a street scene, and every theater had one. So we settled for mine. I'd been carrying this act around for a year. I never could quite get the bulge pressed out of my pocket.

We rehearsed at different publishers' rehearsal rooms, because I didn't have enough money to hire a hall. By telling a series of publishers we were interested in doing their songs, we could get in about three or four hours a day of rehearsals.

These rehearsals always had the benefit of an audience. I brought in everybody: some friends, some acquaintances from Wiennig's, people I'd never seen before, and a few of the waiters. I just wanted an opinion about this girl. I didn't have any—any professional opinion, that is. These people did—about her, and about the act. Their opinions all differed.

They each had ideas about what to do with the act—
also all different. They had only two things in common, none of them were in show business, and none
of them knew what they were talking about. By the
end of three weeks, both Gracie and I were nervous
wrecks. Gracie didn't rehearse well. I don't like to
brag, but I was one of the greatest rehearsers in the
business. I liked this girl, and I knew that she had
been impressed by the way I rehearsed. Now that we
were coming to the end of rehearsal time and about
to face a real live audience, I was terrified that she
would find out the truth about me. I was great in rehearsal halls, but in those days, whatever carries a
performer through left me the minute I got in front
of the footlights. I was just plain bad.

The more uncertain I became about how I felt
about Gracie professionally, the more certain I was
about how I felt about her personally. I never cared
so much about whether I might flop. I just didn't
want her to see me do it. It was a little tough to hide,
because we made all our entrances and exits together.

We were with each other constantly, and it took a
long time to ever really find out anything about
Gracie. She'd talk about the act, the business in general, and about her friends, but she never talked
about herself. I did find out that when she had come
back to see Rena Arnold, she had been going to secretarial school and was about to quit show business.
As in my case, it meant giving up her greatest love.
But the breaks had been bad, and she figured it was
about time to make a change.

I Love Her, That's Why!

She had danced since she was four. (Even here she had the jump on me. If you'll remember, I didn't get into show business until I was seven.) She'd gone to a convent in San Francisco, and it was clear to the sisters even then that this girl had something a little different. She couldn't wait to get out of her uniform and into the top hat and tails she wore to entertain on weekends. Anyway, as soon as she could get out of school and on to a stage, she did. She did an act with her sisters at first, then several different ones with other people, and finally wound up in an act called "Larry Reilly and Company." She was the "and Company." They were booked into the United States Theater in Hoboken, and she arrived and noticed that the billing in front of the theater just said "Larry Reilly"; the "and Company" had been omitted. She quit, and I don't blame her. If your name is "and Company" you want to see it up in lights.

There are lots more stories like this, but I can't get at them. Gracie says I wanted to write a book, so I should write it. She's too busy memorizing forty-three pages of script a week and helping Sandra decorate her new house. (Sandra is my daughter, as I believe I mentioned already. I don't think I've told you much about her yet, but I will.) Anyway, Gracie was ready to join up with anybody, even me, when I came along. It was a choice of secretarial school, teaching dancing back home in S.F., or me. She didn't have train fare home, and hated to type, so my irresistible charm won out.

Our first date was to break in our act at the Hillstreet Theater in Newark, three days, at five dollars a day. We walked into the theater on a day when there was seven or eight inches of snow on the ground. The theater was freezing. The musicians all wore overcoats and gloves, and hopped from one foot to the other. Whether you liked it or not your music was played in double tempo, it was the only way the musicians could keep warm.

In those days, a performer could be closed after one performance. I was waiting to rehearse, watching the manager hang the scenery. It seemed like a good time to strike up a little conversation and get on the right side of him. My favorite act in the world was a man-and-woman act called "Davis and Darnell in 'Birdseeds.' " I thought they were the greatest, and thought everybody in the world knew about them. I figured a little act-dropping wouldn't hurt, so I cleared my throat and hollered:

"Mr. Kennedy, regards from Davis and Darnell!"

He hollered back, "Never heard of them."

Obviously, I made a blunder. Then I noticed that Kennedy was shivering, and I thought of the bottle of gin I had in my dressing room. I'm not a drinking man, but I was so nervous about never having done a talking act before, that I knew I was going to need a little false courage to get the words out. Kennedy was now blue with cold. I walked over to him.

"Mr. Kennedy," I said, "how would you like to have a nice slug of gin?"

He didn't answer me. He just yelled up to the men in the flies: "Hold the scenery, I'll be right back." He followed me down to the dressing room.

As I was pouring him a half a glass of gin, I said,

I Love Her, That's Why!

"Mr. Kennedy, I hope Miss Allen and myself will be a hit in the Number Two spot for you." He put the gin to his lips, said, "Hmmm, good gin," finished it, and said, "You're next to closing."

The dressing rooms in this theater had no ceilings, and you could hear everything that went on in all of them. Just before we went on, there was a crash from Gracie's room, and she cried, "George, I broke a mirror!" Now I may tell you that we were like most show people, deeply superstitious, and we were scared anyway. I tried to make us both feel better by calling back, "That means seven years' good luck." But I said it with my fingers crossed.

In our act I had all the funny lines. After all, I wrote the act myself. I also had a funny costume. I'd seen a picture of Joe E. Brown in the paper, and he was wearing wide pants, a big red bow tie, and a hat turned up in front. This was very funny. So I wore wider pants, a bigger red bow tie, and a hat turned up in front and back, too. Gracie had all the straight questions and I had all the funny answers. We went on, and they laughed at all her questions and at none of my answers. There were only fifteen people in the audience, most of them guys with their sample cases under their seats, who'd just come in to try and get warm, and yet I felt the same thing those fifteen people felt. I felt Gracie's personality. The act was terrible, but as we walked off the stage I knew we were in. And I was right.

I was wrong about those seven years' good luck, though. It's been thirty.

This girl, who rehearsed like nothing, was struck

by something magic in front of an audience. They adored her. Just to show you how hammy a guy can be, I was so excited that I immediately called my agent, Joe Michaels, and said, "I want you to see this act." He said, "I can't get there. There's a blizzard on, remember?" I said, "If you don't make it tonight, I'll give the act to someone else." I want you to remember that we were getting five dollars a day.

It was then, right then, that I knew what to do. Before the next performance I tore the act apart, gave Gracie all the jokes, and took the straight lines. It broke my heart, but I was young, and hungry, and not a dope. That night we were a hit.

After the show we took some friends out to dinner to celebrate. There were the two girls Gracie lived with: Rena Arnold and Mary Kelly—or Pretty Mary Kelly as she was always known. Jack Benny, who was crazy about Mary (Note to Mary Livingston: This was long before you and Jack Benny met), Rena's date, and Gracie and me. It was a great evening because of our success and the fact that we were all such good friends and had so much in common.

Jack and I hit it off right away when we met. I could always make him laugh off stage, and he could always make everybody laugh on. He would have given anything to do what I did, and I would have given my right eye to have his effect on an audience. Jack and I had the same problem too. He was in love with Mary and she was in love with someone else. I was in love with Gracie and she was in love with someone else. Rena Arnold was just in love with her act, and too busy looking for a partner to look for a man. She finally found a partner, then she found the man, married him and left the partner. Anyway, we went out to dinner, and I didn't tell Rena the pineapple story, so everything went well.

The dinner cost fourteen dollars, giving us a profit of one dollar for our three-day run. Correction: Joe Michaels did get through the snow to catch our act, he came backstage and I bought him a corned-beef sandwich. Net profit: forty cents.

We were a really big hit, due in no way to my talents. Rewritten, the act went something like this:

ME: How's your brother?

GRACIE: (*Gracie speaks for five minutes.*)

ME: Is that so?

GRACIE: (*Gracie speaks for five more minutes.*)

ME: A bicycle without a chain?

GRACIE: (*Gracie speaks for three more minutes.*)

ME: No!

Then she did an Irish jig, while I tapped my foot, and we exited. At last I was doing a talking act.

Our next booking was into Boonton, New Jersey, for Farley Marcus. We were late getting to the theater because we couldn't find it. It turned out to be on the second floor. When we walked in, the manager was sitting there with his father. The old man didn't say anything. The manager said, "Where you been?" We explained that we didn't know the place was upstairs, and started looking around. It was a sort of a serve-yourself theater, with folding chairs piled up around the edge of the wall which the audience had to put up for themselves.

The manager said, "What kind of an act do you do?" I said, "A talking act." He said, "But I told Farley Marcus I wanted a singing-dancing act." I said, "Well, that's not what we do; ours is strictly a talking act." "Then you open the show," he said. "If there's anything father hates, it's talk." Father nodded.

After this second-story job, we were booked into the Myrtle Theater in Brooklyn. I was frightened to death, because this was the theater that had the "Love is like the mumps" manager. But we were in luck. He wasn't there any more. Someone had handed him his pictures too.

Gracie was dressing with a girl who used to stand in the middle of the room and shower powder all over herself. She also showered it on Gracie and Gracie's clothes. There were eight clothes hooks in the room. The girl took seven of them. She was a doll. Gracie didn't argue about it. She handled it in her own way. (Her own way then and now is to mind her own business, ask for nothing but what's due her—but just because she's little, *don't* push her around.)

She came in for the evening performance and said to the girl, "We just had dinner with Eddie Darling. He's out front now to catch our act." Eddie Darling was the biggest booker in town.

The girl was beside herself. "Will you please talk to him?" she said. "I want him to catch ours, too."

When Gracie returned to the dressing room after the performance she had seven of the clothes hooks, but the editors said if I said that, it would make

Gracie look selfish. I'm the last one in the world to make Gracie look selfish, so . . . . Gracie had four hooks, the girl had four hooks, and Simon and Schuster are liars.

From the Myrtle we went to the Greenpoint Theater, which was also in Brooklyn. Mamma came backstage to see us after the show, and the three of us went out to dinner. Gracie was darling to her, and I was excited because I could tell that Mamma had taken to Gracie immediately. I was the only one that got much to eat, though, as Mamma wouldn't touch the food because it wasn't kosher, and Gracie was so busy trying to sell me to Mamma that she didn't get a chance to eat. Believe me, it wasn't easy for me to eat three whole dinners.

"Well," Gracie said brightly, "how did you like your son, Mrs. Birnbaum?"

"I think you were wonderful," said Mamma.

"Didn't you think he looked smart in that pinstripe suit?" said Gracie. "He wears his clothes so well, don't you think?"

"I certainly think you do," Mamma said. "You looked beautiful—just beautiful."

Gracie didn't give up easily. "It's such a pleasure working with him," she said. "He's so talented, really funny." She laughed. "You know, I'd better be careful or you're going to get the impression I think he's good."

"He is," said Mamma. "He always has been. At home he always keeps us laughing—singing, dancing—there's nobody so talented. He's a joy around the house."

Gracie said, "He must be. But on the stage—what do you think of him on the stage?"

Mamma said, "On the stage he acts just like some relative got him the job."

In case you are in any doubt about my talent at the time, my mother was always looking to get laughs.

Well, anyway, it was catch-as-catch-can for a while. We played little theaters all over New York, Connecticut, and New Jersey, for about ten weeks. Then we were booked into the Columbia Theater, now the Mayfair, in New York. The billing for the act was, "Burns and Allen in Sixty-Forty." Don't ask me what Sixty-Forty meant; I just liked the sound of it. It sounded sort of like, "Davis and Darnell in 'Birdseeds.' "

The Columbia played burlesque all week except Sunday. On that day they held a Sunday concert that was a showcase for agents and bookers. If they liked the performers they booked them.

Our act opened with Gracie coming on-stage with a spotlight on her, looking for me. I walked on in the dark, lighting a cigar. She saw me, started bawling me out: nobody should have anything to do with me, I'm no good, I'm always late, etc., etc., and at the end of three minutes, she said, "Here I've talked to you for three minutes and you don't even answer me. Aren't you going to say something?"

I turned and looked at her and said, "Hello, Babe." And went back to my cigar.

This line was extremely important, it was either good for a big laugh, or it fell flat on its face. I wor-

93

ried about it so much that I almost worried it to
death. I'd walk down the street saying, "Hello,
Babe," in every possible way. "Hello, Babe—no,
that's not right. *Hello*, Babe. Hello, *Babe!*" and so
on.

People either said hello back or reported me to the
police for trying to get fresh. I finally thought I'd
conquered it, and that afternoon at the Columbia
Theater, we went on and Gracie said, "Why don't
you say something?"

I opened my mouth and absolutely nothing came
out. Not a sound.

Gracie covered for me—up to this point she'd had
all but one line, now she had them all. You know,
they never missed mine. I hate to tell you this: it
didn't hurt the act at all. We did well, and got some
bookings.

For the next five or six months we played the
small Keith time. We were what is termed a "disappointment act," which meant that we stayed home
by the phone waiting for something to happen to
some performer somewhere, a broken leg, or an actor who didn't like his billing, or had missed a train,
or something like that. When it happened, we got
called to replace the act. We were lucky. There were
lots of theaters at that time, and lots of accidents.
This all seems funny now, but it didn't then. We
were fighting for our livelihood, and though we
never wished anyone bad luck, whether someone
tripped or not sometimes meant whether we ate or
not.

Once we were booked into New Haven, and it took

the Yale men to teach me the real meaning of College Humor. We were grateful to them, because we had our job as a result of one of their pranks. What had happened was that a group of students had kidnapped a sister act. They didn't hurt the girls; in fact, they just showed them the town, then returned them, and paid their wages. The girls got a college education, and by the time they arrived back at the theater we had the job.

Though grateful to the Yale men for our job, we were afraid of them as an audience. We were right to be. Just before we made our entrance, the manager came on-stage holding a fire hose, pointed it at the audience, and said, "If there is any more trouble I am turning this on you." He needn't have worried; they were very well behaved; you couldn't hear a thing from them. In fact, you couldn't even see them because, to a man, their faces were behind newspapers which they read throughout our entire act.

I liked being on the road with Gracie. In fact, I liked being anywhere with Gracie. But the road had its advantages. We had to stay in such bad hotels and eat in such bad restaurants in the small towns we played, and Gracie is really a big-town girl anyway, that I figured I looked good in comparison to the surroundings. I also knew it was a good idea to keep her out of New York, because she'd been going with a feller there, and I worked it out that if I was terribly charming, carried her bags, gave her the best lines, etc., by the time we got back to New York he'd be out and I'd be in. I was careful not to let her in on this plot, however, and leaned over backward so she wouldn't know how I felt. This was difficult, because we were together almost all the time.

One part of the act made it particularly tough. I had to say, "What would happen if I gave you a little kiss?" Gracie showed me a whistle on a bracelet and said, "I'd blow this whistle and the police would come." Then I'd kiss her and say, "Why didn't you blow it?" and she'd say, "It's broken from last night."

Now I was so scared she'd find out I was in love with her that this kiss wasn't even a kiss. I barely touched her cheek. It was a stage kiss in every sense of the word. I may not have been much good in the act on tour, but no one has ever given a better performance of a perfect gentleman. I never forgot Rena Arnold's warning: "You remember that Gracie is a good girl—and treat her like a lady, because she is."

After we were booked into New York I began to be really nervous about our relationship. That feller Gracie had been going with started being out front a lot. I was bad anyway, but with him watching me I got worse. One of the first things an actor learns is never to anticipate a cue. I had an entrance where I was supposed to come on-stage, point my finger at Gracie, and say, "You can't get away with that!" I anticipated the cue to such an extent that I walked around backstage for half an hour with my finger stuck out in front of me, waiting to make my entrance.

All my old friends saw the act, and I'd walk down the street and say, "Hello, Mike." He'd say, "Hello, lucky." Then I'd see another friend and say, "Hello, Manny." He'd say, "Hold on to her." And another, "Hello, Dave," and I'd get back, "Sign her—don't let her get away."

Well, this didn't do me any good; it had a terrific effect on me. I was in an awful spot. It was now obvious to everybody that she was great and I was lousy. Gracie did everything to make me feel better, and it must have been tough, because she was undoubtedly getting remarks from her friends, too. Like, "Where did you pick *him* up?" "How did you get stuck with that?"—that sort of thing. But she never let on—just told me I was great in the act, was kind and courteous to me, asked my advice to make me feel important; but it didn't do any good. My problem was, I knew she was really interested in somebody else.

What with being called lucky, and walking around stiff-fingered, and that guy out front, I took to walking home down alleys and having long talks with myself. Among other things I said I really didn't care about Gracie; it was just that the act was going so well I didn't want to lose her as a partner. I also said, what was I doing in show business anyway? It was a lousy racket, and not worth all the heartaches involved in it. Then one night, as I was walking home kicking at cans, which didn't make me feel any better, it came to me.

All my life I'd been in love with show business, and now, for the first time, I loved something more. Well, there was nothing wrong with that. It might be temporarily confusing, but why couldn't it be

97

worked out? From that night on, I got better in the act. This may have been because I was finally facing facts; on the other hand, it may have been because I couldn't have gotten worse. You strike bottom, and there is no place to go but up. I got so much better, in fact, that when I was on-stage with Gracie, pretty soon they didn't notice me at all.

Then we were booked into the Fifth Avenue Theater, another showcase where, if you had improved since they'd last seen you, the agents booked you into better theaters. We were a hit. This was a step up. We were now a de luxe disappointment act. We were packed and waiting for someone to break a leg, when the phone rang and we were called to the Bushwick Theater in Brooklyn to replace an act called "Ward and Irving."

This was our first big time—a two-a-day, which we never played before. Nora Bayes was headliner. We were a riot. We were such a hit that the following week we were booked into the Orpheum Theater in Brooklyn, and we weren't replacing anyone. The headliner was Ethel Barrymore, who was doing "The Twelve Pound Look" in vaudeville.

We were so excited that we weren't replacing anyone, and that we were in such impressive company, that we took a quarter-page ad in *Variety* so everyone would know about it. We were on next to closing, following Miss Barrymore. Everybody came to see Ethel Barrymore before she returned to the legitimate theater. They saw her; she went off; they went out; we came on; and we played to their backs as they left.

We never got a laugh, so the manager moved us up to the Number Two spot. Our world collapsed. In this place all the people who came to see Miss Barrymore were just coming in and taking off their overcoats and settling down. They never really saw us while we were on. We never got a laugh there either. We stayed in our dressing rooms throughout the entire run, had our meals there, and never came out until the rest of the players had left the theater at night. We never even read our ad in *Variety*.

This sounds sad. It was. We went back to being a disappointment act for a couple of months, and finally were booked into Hertig and Seeman's Theater on 125th Street for another Sunday concert.

On the bill with us was a man named General Pissano who did a shooting act, which was the last act on the bill. The act next to closing was a nut comedian called Harry Breen who wore a derby hat on the side of his head. He was great. He stayed on-stage for twenty-five minutes, and the audience didn't want him to leave then. Sunday night, Pissano had to leave because he was engaged in Syracuse for a week. He said to Breen, "When you do your last show tonight, if you stay on the stage more than eighteen minutes I'll miss my train."

"Okay," said Breen, "signal me when the eighteen minutes is up, and I'll go into my exit."

Breen went out, and he was a riot. He forgot all about General Pissano, who was standing in the wings. When the eighteen minutes was up, Pissano looked at his watch and signaled to Breen. Breen was killing them, and paid no attention. Pissano

99

waved his handkerchief, but he still couldn't get Breen's attention. Pissano picked up his gun and shot him through the derby. Breen said, "Good night, everybody." Pissano made his train.

At this same theater we had our first fight. It was close to being the last. It all happened before the matinee. I knocked on Gracie's dressing-room door and was so excited that I banged on the door and yelled at the same time.

"Gracie, believe it or not, I've just okayed a contract to play the Cosmos Theater in Washington for four hundred and fifty dollars a week."

I was waiting for her to faint or something, we'd never made more than $300 before. She said through the door, "Call them back and cancel it."

I thought she'd lost her mind. "You're kidding," I said, trying to control myself. "Gracie, *listen*. The salary is four hundred and fifty a week!"

Very quietly she said, "Call them back and cancel it."

I was in no mood for anyone to underplay anything and cancel $450 at the same time, so I said, "I'd like to remind you, Gracie, that a verbal contract is as binding as a written one. It's either play, or pay the four hundred and fifty dollars—and you know I haven't got four dollars and fifty cents." This time there was no answer. "Gracie!" I yelled. "I okayed this date!"

The door opened a crack. "I've got a few dollars," she said. "I'll pay it, but I won't play it."

I started to scream, "But we're headlining the bill—"

100

"That's worse," she said. "Then everyone will know we're there."

I was frozen. Never, I think, in my whole life had I been so angry. I called the agent, gave him a cock-and-bull story he didn't believe, but he released us from the commitment. I came back to make my entrance in a cold fury. Who the hell did this dame think she was, anyway? Sheer pig-headed Irish stubbornness would make her break up our act—$450 and she wouldn't even say why. O.K., break up the act. Who needed her anyway? Four hundred and fifty dollars!

I looked at her waiting for me to go on—tiny, straight figure, the light on her hair, small foot tapping. I wanted to shake her or kiss her, I couldn't tell which, but they were playing our entrance music —$450! As we went on, I said, "Well, I got out of the date." She didn't answer. We made our entrance, and were struck by that wonderful wave of feeling that comes up when you have a great audience. It's what keeps performers alive. If your audience is good, the hotel you're staying in is good, the food is good, everything is good. The people were just great. They loved us, and because of that, when we came off we didn't talk about splitting up any more.

Gracie said, "You were great, Nat." I gulped. Between the stage and the dressing room I went from deciding to forgive her to hoping she'd forgive me. As I opened her dressing-room door for her— yes I did—she turned to me and said, "Nat, I'm sorry about the Cosmos Theater. It is a small-time theater that does five shows a day—I played it with

101

I Love Her, That's Why!

Larry Reilly. I wouldn't mind that, but my sister Hazel's husband is in the diplomatic service in Washington—he's just getting started—and if Hazel saw us billed in that theater she might be embarrassed and have to start making excuses for us. Now please don't think it has anything to do with the act—I was afraid you might think I was ashamed of it, that's why I didn't tell you before we went on. I'm not. It's a *good* act! How about that last performance?—they loved us, didn't they?"

I said, "Didn't they? . . . You know, Gracie, a few minutes ago I was saying to myself, 'Who needs her? I don't. I got along before I met her; I can get along without her now.' That's what I said. But you can't go by what I say. I'm a terrible liar."

As I started out to my dressing room Gracie said, "Nattie—"

I said, "Yes."

She said, "You're not a liar, and I need you, too."

Six months later we didn't need two dressing rooms. We were married.

10

NEXT we were booked for nineteen weeks on the Loew's circuit. We were now in Small Big Time. We changed the name of the act to "Dizzy," which came from part of the dialogue, most of which I won't bother you with. But just so you get an idea—

ME: You're dizzy.

GRACIE: I'm glad I'm dizzy. Boys like dizzy girls and I like boys.

ME: I'm glad you're glad you're dizzy.

GRACIE: I'm glad you're glad, I'm glad, etc., etc.

Well, that's why it was called "Dizzy."

New Year's Eve we were playing Loew's 86th Street. The act opened with me on stage talking to the orchestra leader. It went something like this:

ME: This little book I'm carrying is a book of systems.

ORCHESTRA LEADER: What kind of systems?

ME: All kinds. How to win at horses, how to meet a girl—everything.

ORCHESTRA LEADER: How would you meet a girl?

I Love Her, That's Why!

ME: You take an impossible name like Mamie Dittenfest, then you go up to a girl and say, "Pardon me, aren't you Mamie Dittenfest?" She'll say no. You say, "Well, you certainly look like her." She'll say, "I'm not, though," then the next thing you know you're buying her a cup of coffee.

Then Gracie made her entrance, and I said to the orchestra leader, "Watch this. . . . I beg your pardon, is your name Mamie Dittenfest?" and she said "Yes." This was what you call a shock laugh. Then I would start to walk out fast and she followed me.

New Year's Eve, however, the audience made so much noise with horns and ratchets and other noise-makers that nobody heard me talk to the leader or to Gracie. I said, "Is your name Mamie Dittenfest?" She said "Yes." Nobody heard us. I walked off. She followed me. I walked straight to my dressing room, and Gracie to hers. The act lasted thirty seconds.

After playing the 86th Street, we went on tour for the other eighteen weeks in and around New York. During the time we were on the Loew's circuit, I kept playing the gentleman. The other feller was still hovering, and I wasn't taking any chances of tipping my hand at the wrong time. We saw a lot of Mary Kelly and Jack Benny. This was good, because Mary liked me and was trying to persuade Gracie that she was going with the wrong feller. We all had so much in common that we even shared the same agent. His name was Tom Fitzpatrick and he had offices in the Palace Theater Building. He was a very fine man and extremely kind. In fact, he was so kind he couldn't bear to tell an actor he didn't

104

have a job for him. If someone came in, and he had bad news, he put his head way down in a desk drawer and pretended to be looking for something. He kept opening and closing drawers and looking into them during the interview, and never looked up until the actor went away.

I came out of the building one day and ran into Jack Benny. He said, "Are you working next week?" I said, "No, Fitzpatrick just gave me the drawer routine." Jack started to laugh. I didn't know what he thought was so funny—Fitzpatrick gave everybody the drawer routine. I said, "What are you laughing at?" For some reason this made him laugh harder. So I stopped some strangers going by and said, "Do you know why this man is laughing?" They said, "Don't you?" I said, "No." By this time Jack was screaming, and I was gathering more people. Pretty soon there must have been a couple of hundred people standing in a circle staring at him. This made him laugh so hard he fell down on the ground. Finally he crawled into a shoe store and just lay there on the floor gasping.

I don't know why I tell you this except that it proves why my friendship with Jack is on such a firm basis. I'm not letting go of anyone who laughs that easily.

Speaking of laughter and of making jokes, I've always had a theory about them. The minute you say to someone, "I said a funny thing last night," you're dead. Automatically he's not going to think it's funny. This theory proved itself to me when I did say something funny to Joe Frisco. I just had to

tell it around, so I said George Jessel said it. This
way I had two things going for myself: I didn't say
I said it; and if it laid an egg it was Jessel's. This
would have been fine except it turned out to be really
funny and was all over Broadway for three months.
Jessel was so pleased with it that he got to thinking
he had said it. I ran into him one day and he said,
"Did you hear what I said to Joe Frisco?"

I said, "*You* didn't say that."

He said, "That's right. You did."

I said, "That's right."

While we were on the Loew's circuit, we worked
on the act, added jokes, I learned more about writing
Gracie's part, and we gradually purified the zany
character that Gracie has played ever since. I say
purified, which is really the wrong word, because
Gracie had an instinct for the characterization the
first time she walked on a stage. Contrary to opinion, Gracie is not a comedienne. She is an extremely
good straight dramatic actress. It is the situations
that are funny. The character she plays has what we
call "illogical logic." She is completely earnest about
what she is doing and saying, and I think it is the
fact that she is so kind to the rest of the world for
its lack of understanding of what is perfectly clear
to her that makes people love her. She is right and
everybody else is wrong, but she doesn't blame them
—she just gently tries to explain to them, patiently,
and puts up with everybody.

While we were on the Loew's circuit, jokes started
out by being something like this:

ME: I'm a pauper.

106

GRACIE: Congratulations. Boy or girl?

That grew up into:

GRACIE: My sister had a baby.

ME: Boy or girl?

GRACIE: I don't know, and I can't wait to find out if I'm an aunt or uncle.

Then we went into a stylized mad form of humor that went this way:

GRACIE: My brother has a suit like that. It's just the same.

ME: Is that so?

GRACIE: Yes, only his hasn't any stripes. His is brown. It's more like a blue black, sort of yellow.

ME: More like white.

GRACIE: That's it. A white suit, only yours is double-breasted and his is single-breasted and has no pockets, and a bow on the side.

ME: A *bow* on the side?

GRACIE: My sister wore it to a dance last night.

ME: Your sister wore your brother's suit to a dance?

GRACIE: I haven't got a brother.

ME: You haven't got a brother but your sister has?

GRACIE: It's a long story—pull up a chair. You see, when my sister and I were children, we were left orphans, and he was one of them.

You see, the insanity was established fairly early.

While we were on the Loew's circuit, I continued to play the part of a gentleman, but I wasn't kidding anybody about the way I felt about Gracie, particularly Gracie. She knew. She was terribly nice to me,

107

but she still had her eye on the other feller; so I held back, kept on with the stage kiss, carried her bags, gave her the best lines, and waited for my cue.

After we got back to New York we received a wire offering us twenty weeks on the Orpheum circuit. This was absolute tops. We'd never had a better offer. I signed the contracts, started to get things in order to leave, and then, just four days before we were supposed to go, that certain feller arrived back in town. He said Gracie shouldn't put him off any longer; she should break up the act and marry him right away.

Gracie didn't know what to do. Her lifelong ambition had been to play the Orpheum Theater in San Francisco, and she also didn't want to let me down, but this feller was very insistent. She went to Mary Kelly (bless her) with her problem and told her she was about to break up the act. Mary said she thought it was unfair. She said Gracie was not only breaking up the act, she was breaking my heart too. Obviously I was in love with her and too much of a gentleman to say so while the other feller was around (at least I had convinced *her*). She then said that if Gracie was going to do it, to let me down easy.

She said, "Why not do this: Tell George that three hundred and fifty dollars a week is not enough, that you think the act is worth more, and that you won't play the Orpheum circuit unless the act gets a fifty-dollar raise. You know the booker won't give it to you and that will give you an out. And it's nicer than just saying, 'I'm breaking up the act, good-by.'"

When Gracie phoned me and gave me the story, I knew she was looking for an out. But there was nothing for me to do but try the impossible. I made my way to the Orpheum offices with that dropping-elevator feeling in my stomach. I knew what was going to happen. This was the end of Burns and Allen. While I was on my way over to the offices, Mary Kelly called Ray Myers, who was the booker at the Orpheum, and who, you'll remember, was mad about her. She said, "George Burns is on his way over to ask for a fifty-dollar raise. If you don't give it to him I'll never see you again." And she hung up.

I walked in, and before I had a chance to open my mouth, Ray said, "Okay, you win. The act is getting four hundred dollars a week."

As I left, I couldn't find the doorknob. When I recovered, I staggered into a phone booth and called Gracie. She was stuck. Mary Kelly wrote her some dialogue for the other feller that went something like:

"We've waited so long to be married, we can wait twenty weeks longer."

It didn't go well, and the day before we left Gracie tried one more out. She said, "I can't go; my trunk isn't big enough." Well, this time I didn't wait for Mary Kelly. I bought a trunk—a big one—and carried it on my back from Forty-fourth to Forty-seventh Street in a heavy snowstorm. She couldn't think of anything else, and said she'd go.

The next day I was at the station, complete with tickets, baggage, and Benny—waiting for her. It got closer and closer to train time and she didn't appear. Jack was pacing up and down with me. He had come to see us off, and he tried not to let me know that he thought maybe Gracie wouldn't show. Jack kept biting his nails and saying, "George, don't be nervous; she'll be here. I'm sure she'll be here. Don't be nervous. She'll be here, really she will. Stop being nervous." Just as the train was pulling out, Gracie ran down the platform. We jumped on, waved good-by to Jack. We were gone, and so were Jack Benny's nails.

I was so relieved that Gracie had arrived that my relief turned into anger. I knew where she'd been. As we stood on the train platform to catch our breath, I said, "You were gone long enough to marry him—why didn't you?" She just said very quietly, "Stop the train and I will." She was underplaying it again. I got so mad, and I got so mean, and I was so brave because I had her on the train, that I grabbed her by the shoulder and started to shake her. Then something happened and I kissed her instead. I forgot about being a gentleman, and it wasn't a stage kiss.

She gave me a funny look, but she only said, "Will you please help me with my bags?—we may be in someone's way here." I carried the bags into her compartment, and Gracie turned to me and said, "Now I dare you to shake me again." I did. I shook her and I kissed her again. Before I left the compartment I shook her four times. Eight weeks later I kissed her without shaking her.

11

OUR arrival in Winnipeg for the start of the Orpheum tour didn't do anything to improve the already strained relations between Gracie and me. We were extremely polite to each other, and as you know, that's the most dangerous sign. She didn't quite know what she wanted to do about me, and I knew exactly what I wanted to do about her. We talked about the weather a lot, and it was something to talk about. It was terrible—and so was our billing. When we arrived at the theater we found we were on Number Two, and I don't have to tell you again that that is the worst spot on the bill for a talking act. The miserable part of this particular billing was that on the Orpheum circuit, if you're on Number Two in Winnipeg, you're on Number Two for the entire tour.

I was afraid this might really tear it, as far as Gracie was concerned. To give up a marriage because I tricked her into going on tour was one thing. To give up a marriage and find herself on Number

Two in Winnipeg was liable to be impossible. She never beefed when we saw where we were billed; she was just very quiet and ladylike. But before she had a chance to say anything, I said, "Look, I'll see what I can do about it. I can't refuse to play—it's play or pay, but I'll tell the manager something, say you're sick, maybe. You go back to the hotel and lie down." I went to the manager and said Gracie didn't feel well.

He said, "Then you go on alone." I said that I couldn't do that, then he said, "Where can I get another act in Winnipeg? This is ridiculous!" He was looking at the blackboard as he was talking. Then he suddenly said, "Wait a minute! That billing is wrong! Right after the opening act, it's supposed to be the two girls who sing on Number Two; Al K. Hall third; then Burns and Allen fourth; Robert Warwick fifth; then Joe Frisco; then the big act."

I didn't know whether he was setting a trap for me. I said, "Are you sure that's right?" He called an usher and showed me a program. The billing was in that order. I called Gracie right in front of him and said, "Gracie, put the hot-water bottle away; we're on Number Four."

The Orpheum tour took us to Calgary, Vancouver, Seattle, Portland, and then to San Francisco, going out. Then we were to work back to New York the other way, starting at Denver. As we got closer to San Francisco, Gracie grew more excited. It was her home; her family was there, and her childhood ambition had been to play the Orpheum. In fact, she had been such a stage-struck child that the only way her mother could get her to remember directions was to give them in their proximity to theaters. She'd say, "Go to the gas company and pay the bill. You go two blocks past the Orpheum, and it's just this side of the Alcazar."

Gracie was looking forward with such excitement to playing the Orpheum that I thought that was what was making her sick when we played Oakland the week before. It wasn't. It was appendicitis. To make a long story sad, the week she should have been on the Orpheum stage she was in a hospital bed. It was a terrible disappointment to her, but it was the best appendicitis I ever met. I visited her every day in the hospital and, after the operation, in her home. I took her flowers, brought in some new stories, and made up some new lies. I was even a hit. I'm sorry to say she even broke a few stitches laughing at me. And to make everything more rosy, her family liked me, her nurses thought I was a riot, and she wasn't hearing from the other feller. He was mad at her for not marrying him; she was mad at him for not writing her. I wasn't mad at anybody. I was enjoying a beautiful convalescence.

On the way back to New York, I grew even more charming. I took her dancing, sent her flowers, bought her presents, and when we finished the Orpheum circuit I owed her four hundred dollars.

Back in New York it was Christmas week, and I was full of joy. I thought I was in, the other feller was out, and I was working on a new act—what more does a guy want for Christmas? The new act was called "Lambchops" and was based on the same

113

joke that everything of the year was: a man takes a girl out to dinner and she eats him out of all his money. A friend of mine, a fine writer named Al Boasberg, wrote the act. We were happy with the way it seemed to be developing, and felt it was a definite improvement over "Dizzy." We were booked on the Gus Sun circuit for five weeks, starting after Christmas. I didn't tell Sun he was getting a tryout of a new act. He thought he was getting "Dizzy." After Gracie and I signed the contracts, we were in a cab on our way to doing some Christmas shopping.

I said, "What if we go out and do a little celebrating tonight?"

She said, "I'd love to, but I'm afraid I can't—I have a date." I knew right away who it was. He must have gotten back into town without my knowing it. I'd been lulled into a false sense of security and it made me furious. I was so mad, I could have sworn, but I decided this time *I* was going to underplay it.

"Driver," I said, "pull over to the curb. I guess this is where I get out." She didn't say anything. Not even "Good-by."

I had a miserable evening. I went to Wiennig's. The phone rang any number of times, and I never even threw one piece of sugar. The next night the three girls, Gracie, Mary Kelly, and Rena Arnold had a Christmas party at their apartment. I was supposed to be Santa Claus and give out the presents. I had the costume, including a blue beard which I thought would get a few laughs. I told you I was a riot at sociables. The props were there but the spirit wasn't.

114

Benny was waiting for me to be funny. I wasn't. Unless you call giving everybody the wrong presents being funny. I just couldn't get off the ground. I watched Gracie across the room waiting for her to open my package. I had bought her a bracelet with one tiny diamond in it. My plan had been to add one every year we were together. I wished I had given her a bottle of perfume instead. What was I doing— planning for a future when there wasn't any? Mary knew I was unhappy and tried to cheer me up, which only made me feel worse. Jack tried to make me feel better by telling *me* jokes. I didn't laugh, and that made him feel worse.

Then Gracie opened the bracelet. She was full of enthusiasm. She came over to me and thanked me. She was darling. I wasn't. The next package I took out of the bag was Gracie's present to me. I read the card out loud:

" 'To Nat—all my love.' *Ha-ha-ha!*" I snarled nastily. In fact, I was perfectly terrible. I was so terrible that I made her cry. I never even lent her my handkerchief. She ran out of the room and shut herself in the bathroom.

Rena said, "Well, how do you like that? Is she going to spoil the party?"

Mary Kelly said, "Some Christmas spirit."

I turned on them and laid them out properly. "How dare you?" I said. "That poor little girl listens to all *your* troubles. Now the minute she has a problem herself, you complain. Some friends you are." I walked out and knocked on the bathroom door. I could hear snuffling through the door. I said, "Listen, Gracie, we've got five weeks on the Gus Sun time to break in our new act. After the second week, we have a three-day layoff. In that three days, we either get married, or it's good-by." I paused, and with perfect timing pulled my beard off, hung it on the door, and made my exit. You've heard of a white Christmas. This was a black one.

I lay in bed that night, bitterly reviewing my life. After all these years of work and striving, I finally had an act almost as good as "Birdseeds." I'd found a girl I was mad about; she was beautiful and talented, and I had thought she was almost mine. Now here it was Christmas, and I was alone in a hotel room with nothing but an empty Santa Claus suit to keep me company.

Then at three o'clock in the morning the phone rang. It was Gracie. She said, "Before we leave Monday for the Gus Sun time, you'd better buy the ring."

When I could say anything, I said, "How did you make up your mind it was me and not the other feller?"

She said, "Because it was you who made me cry. I figured if you could make me cry, I must be in love with you. After you left, I called him and broke the date. He was very nice; asked me to call him later. I spent all evening thinking about us. A few minutes ago, he called again and said, 'I've been waiting all evening—why didn't you call me?' I said, 'I—I don't know.' He said, 'Look—don't you love me?' I said, 'I—I guess not.' He said, 'Please hang up.' And I did."

Fourteen days later Gracie was wearing the ring.

116

"Lambchops"

12

I WENT straight to Mamma to tell her the news. I was almost sure she'd be happy about it, but a few things worried me. I got it out right away as I walked into the house—before even "Hello." "Mamma," I said, "Gracie and I are going to be married." She looked up from her sewing. "Oh," she said. "So now she loves you too. It took a long time, didn't it, son?" "Yes," I said, "but Mamma, there's one thing I have to talk to you about. Gracie's a Catholic, and I'm a Jew, and—" "Well," she interrupted, "if her mother doesn't mind, I think it's wonderful."

So I bought the ring. I was able to get it wholesale from a friend I'd known when I was in the garment business. It was a thirty-five-dollar ring, and I got it for fifteen. Gracie still wears it. She's picked up a few sparkly things to go with it, now. As a matter of fact, she has enough so she can change them around a little, but the ring she never takes off.

We started out on the Gus Sun circuit, supposedly

doing "Dizzy," but actually we were slipping in a little more of "Lambchops" every performance. Finally we got so mixed up that one afternoon we did all of "Dizzy" and all of "Lambchops" and couldn't get off.

The manager gave us a terrible bawling out. "Listen," he said, "if I'd wanted an act to stay on stage thirty-two minutes I'd have hired a Fanchon and Marco Unit."

This didn't dampen our spirits. Nothing could have. I was walking on air. The pressure was off—Gracie was going to be mine. I got more relaxed in the act; and as I became less of a gentleman, I became more of an actor. In between shows we sat in the dressing room and worked on the act and talked. It was wonderful, after keeping still so long, to have someone to talk to about Gracie. Especially when the person was Gracie.

There were no windows in the dressing rooms, but the sunlight streamed in. The two weeks on the road before we were married was a preamble to a honeymoon. We worked hard on the act—after all, our future was at stake, and at night after the show we went dancing. Here I was sure of myself. It was one thing I knew I was good at, and I gained more confidence by displaying the talent for Gracie.

The audiences were great; the small towns seemed big; the hotels were fine; the food was first-rate—even the ketchup seemed like a vintage brand. When I started to share the same powder puff with Gracie, I knew everything was going to be all right.

The night before we were to leave for Cleveland

to be married, we were walking out the front door of the theater carrying our grips. The theater was dark except for one work light on the stage. They were taking down the scenery. From way backstage, the manager called, "Hey, Burns." I called back, "Yeah?" He said, "Lots of luck tomorrow." I said, "What?" He said, "Am I right?" I said, "You're damned right." I still don't know how he found out. We hadn't told anybody. I guess some of the sunlight must have rubbed off on us.

We'd traveled this far on a cloud, but the rest of the road to Cleveland was on a milk train where we had to sit up all night. It arrived in Cleveland at five in the morning. I had made reservations at the Statler Hotel to spend our three-day honeymoon. When we went to the hotel, we found we'd have to pay for another day unless we waited until seven o'clock for the room. This meant eight dollars. We may have been happy but we weren't foolish. We sat in the hotel lobby for two hours, Gracie asleep with her head on my shoulder.

At seven my brother I. H. (the original George) and his wife Madge, a couple of their friends, and Mary Kelly arrived. They had made arrangements for us with a justice of the peace. We already had a license. This was the angriest justice of the peace you ever saw. As we walked in, he was walking out to go fishing. I said, "Please, just marry us before you go." He said, "Okay, let's get this over with. I'm in a hurry." He certainly was. When we went into his house for the ceremony our cab meter read seventy cents. When we came out, it read ninety.

119

We had a large wedding breakfast back at the Statler. Gracie and I kept yawning, because we'd been up all night. All our friends thought we were hinting, and paid no attention. After all, they'd come a long way to see us, and they were going to make sure they saw us. They stayed with us all day. I tried to be funny, but I was too tired and it didn't come off. Finally they left us and we went up to our room.

At two in the morning the phone woke us. It was Jack Benny, from Vancouver. I recognized his voice. He said, "Hello, George." I said, "Send up another order of ham and eggs," and hung up. Half an hour later he called back. "Hello, George." I said, "And another pot of coffee," and hung up again. When he called back the third time, I let him congratulate us.

We had a wonderful three-day honeymoon in Cleveland, and then we were booked into the Colonial Theater in Detroit. By this time we had removed all of the original "Dizzy" routine except the basic " 'You're dizzy' . . . 'I'm glad I'm dizzy, etc.' " bit. This always got such a big laugh that I couldn't think of changing it. The day after we opened, I ran into a friend and said, "How do you like our new act?" He said, "I've always liked it. What do you mean 'new'?" I said, "But this is a whole different act." "Not to me, it isn't," he said. I couldn't sleep that night, until suddenly it came to me. People remember your big jokes, never the little ones. It's all right to repeat a small joke, but never a big joke.

120

This man only remembered the big one which was "Dizzy." I took it out. It was like pulling a good tooth, but I knew it had to be done. We now had an act billed "Dizzy" which was in reality "Lambchops." If you think you're confused, you should have seen me then.

The last week on the Gus Sun time we got a wire from Tom Fitzpatrick which said: "First half of next week you play Keith's Syracuse doing 'Lambchops.'" Gracie was worried, we were now doing a whole new act, and we'd taken out our funniest routine. Before I kissed her goodnight I said, "Don't worry, Googie." (This is what I call her—forgot to tell you. It was because one night Gracie couldn't sleep, and she said, "I can't sleep. Say something funny." Now at two in the morning my repertoire is limited, so I just mumbled "Googie, googie, googie." Somehow this made Gracie laugh and somehow that became her name. Silly, isn't it?) Anyway, I said, "Don't worry, Googie; one thing, we can always go back to 'Dizzy.' Good night."

"Well," she said, "I'm glad we're sneaking the new act into Syracuse. If it flops, at least not very many people will know it. Good night, Nat." (That's what she calls me—forgot to tell you that too.)

When we arrived at the theater, we found our name up in lights. It seems the manager was a friend of Mary Kelly's and Rena Arnold's, and he was doing us a favor. It was nice of him, but we were much more frightened than pleased. We didn't think we were entitled to the billing, were still very uncertain of the act, and just wanted very little attention paid to us until we were more sure of ourselves.

Well, to make a long story a happy one, we went on, and we were a riot. The audience loved us, and so did the manager. And I didn't think our billing was good enough. The manager called the Keith's booking office in New York and said, "This is a great act. See them and sign them before somebody else does." Tom Fitzpatrick wired us that we were booked into the Jefferson Theater in New York for the last half of that same week. This was more frightening than having our name in lights. The Jefferson was the toughest theater in New York. There was no halfway measure with its audiences. They either loved you or hated you. If they loved you, they wouldn't let you get off; if they didn't, they'd take you off.

We were both terribly nervous the day we opened. The audience was not only tough but full of bookers. If they didn't like the new act, it could affect our whole future. That afternoon Gracie went to her church, St. Malachy's, to light a couple of candles— one for her and one for me. After all, we were a two act.

I went to Wiennig's and threw some sugar with the boys, just to show them that Syracuse hadn't gone to my head.

That night as they were playing our entrance music, I kissed Gracie and said, "Don't worry, sweetheart, we can always go back to 'Dizzy.'" We were an even bigger hit than in Syracuse. We had four or five curtain calls and two encores, and when we came off after the last encore, I was called to the booking office and offered a five-year contract ranging from $450 to $600 a week. I didn't dicker. I signed the contracts. We had only been married three and a half weeks. What a wedding present! The next week I paid Gracie back the $400 and had another stone set in her bracelet.

You may be thinking that this book is beginning to have what they call in script terms "no conflict." That means things keep getting better and better, and nothing happens to keep the boy and girl apart or get in the way of their goal. Well, that's the way it was, and I'm sorry, but unless I can think of a lie before the end of this chapter, that's the way it's going to be.

I can't.

Six weeks later we played the Palace.

It's a Funny Thing about the Palace

13

OUR new success went to our heads and we moved into two rooms. We now had a living room also. I started to wear spats again but these didn't have any buttons missing. I also carried a cane.

We played all the good theaters around, but never got the bid from the Palace we'd been hoping for. After whatever shows we were doing every night, Gracie and I, Mary and Jack Benny, Blossom Seely and Benny Fields, Mary Kelly and Ray Myers, and Jesse Block and Eva Sully all met at one another's houses. I mean hotel rooms. Mary and Ray were the only ones who had a house. As if all of us hadn't acted enough all day (Ray was the only one who wasn't an actor; he was a booker), as soon as the girls fixed us something to eat, we'd all start over. We gave shows for our wives and Ray, and no players ever had a better audience. Especially me. Gracie was, and still is, the best audience a man ever had. I just killed her.

It's a Funny Thing about the Palace

At the start of the show I'd peek out from behind some lace curtains to count the house, and she'd scream. Every night I did it, and every night she screamed. Incidentally, she still laughs up the jokes that she's heard all her life. We all laughed so hard at each other, and the screaming got so loud, that it was practically a nightly occasion to have the house detective threaten to put us out. The funny part of these evenings of hilarity was that no drinking was involved. We'd have an occasional one, but the loudness was due to the fact that we all just plain broke each other up.

Once, at one o'clock in the morning, when we were living, I think, at the Edison Hotel, we were on the fourth floor and the Bennys on the ninth (he was already coming up in the world), I went down to our apartment to put on a costume. For some reason I was about to go on as Huckleberry Finn. I managed to get quite a good costume together—rolled-up pants, bare feet with bandaged toe, shirttails out, Gracie's straw beach hat, and a curtain rod for a fishing pole. If I say so myself, Tom Sawyer couldn't have told me from the original. I was sneaking up the back stairs so as not to be seen, when I ran smack into the house detective. Remember, we'd had trouble with him before. He took a look at me, folded his arms, and said, "Where are *you* going?"

I started to stammer, and at that moment Gracie, who had saved me before and has since, came looking for me and heard what he said. I've told you before what a lady she is—very dignified, this girl. "Where does it look as if he's going?" she said haughtily. "He's going fishing, of course. We're on our way up to Jack Benny's to borrow some worms." She grabbed my hand and we both ran up the stairs, into the Bennys' apartment, slammed the door, told them the story, and the screaming started again.

One night we were playing Proctor's Mt. Vernon, where the headliner was a feller called Harry Fox. Just before we went on for the supper show, the manager came back and said Eddie Darling was out front to catch Fox's act. This was horrible. Darling, the biggest booker in the business, was going to see us play to thirty or forty people. The supper show was called that because that's where everyone was—at supper.

It's tough to play to an almost empty house. This night it was tougher because we could see Darling's face as if he'd been spotlighted.

We went on, did a quiet act, got a few quiet snickers, took a quiet bow, and tiptoed back to our dressing room.

The next day we received a wire from Tom Fitzpatrick saying we'd been booked into the Palace. Darling liked us—after seeing us under the worst possible conditions. Obviously he was a man of taste who knew talent when he saw it—or have I said enough?

The Monday matinee that we opened at the Palace there was a large group of friends out front: Mary Kelly; Rena Arnold; Jack Benny; Orry Kelly, whose name was then Jack Kelly; Cary Grant, whose name was Archie Leach; Al Burns; Blossom Seely and Benny Fields, Block and Sully. They all chipped in

126

five dollars apiece and ordered fifty dollars' worth of flowers for us.

Now, I was petrified, didn't know how we were going to go over, and was so nervous I was twitching. Remember, it was the Palace. But when Mary Kelly said, "When do you want the flowers sent up?" I said, "After the second encore." An actor's ego is a wonderful thing. I never knew I said it until Mary told me, years later.

Well, you'd have thought this group of friends was going on instead of us. They were all so nervous. I had told them, "The important moment is our opening laugh. When the stranger comes on stage, kisses Gracie, exits, and Gracie says, 'George, who was that?'—for God's sake, laugh!" Well, everybody in the audience did laugh, except those ten friends. *They* were frozen.

Now there's a funny thing about the Palace. If you were the headliner you had to make good on your own. If you were any other act on the bill, you couldn't flop. The theater was full of actors. They knew your life was at stake. The toughest thing about the Palace was to book it.

A curious thing happened to me. After all my terrors before the performance, I walked out on the stage and wasn't the slightest bit nervous; and Gracie, who never is, was. They were great to us. We got to stay on until our flowers were brought up, and longer. We were a hit, and the rest of the week I should have been completely relaxed. Instead, *then* I got nervous. I got worse with every performance, and Gracie got better. Finally, just as we were going

127

on, on our last day Gracie said, "Nattie, relax, darling. We can always go back to 'Dizzy.' "

We didn't have to. We now had two rooms, I had new pearl buttons on my spats, a silver tip on my cane, Gracie had three stones in her bracelet; and four months later we sailed for Europe.

The Bird That Flies Backward

14

UNDER the terms of our Keith's contract we were free to accept outside offers for seven out of the fifty-two weeks of the year. When we received an offer to play four out of five weeks in London for $1,600, I turned it down because it seemed to me to be ridiculous. The boat fare over was $1,200. A net profit of $400 didn't appeal to me. It did to Gracie—she was crazy to go. She always had a tremendous enthusiasm and curiosity about other places and people, and she wanted to see Europe. I guess she figured what we lost financially we would gain culturally. With me it was different. If people and places weren't on the Orpheum circuit, they weren't on the map. I was more interested in cash than culture, and wanted to stay home. So, as I made all the decisions, we booked passage on the *Leviathan*.

At least it was progress. This time it was "Call them back and accept," instead of "Call them back and cancel."

We had to buy a few clothes; not many—we didn't have enough money saved up. The day before we sailed, Gracie and I had both been shopping. I finished before her and went home to the hotel to pack. As I approached our room, I noticed the door was slightly ajar. I thought it was the maid and walked right in. It wasn't the maid. It was a robber. He was deeply engrossed in piling our possessions into a sack on the floor.

He heard me come in and turned quickly toward me. I've never been so surprised. It was Mouse Myers, an old friend from the East Side.

"Why, Mouse," I said, "what are you doing here?"

"What does it look like I'm doing?" he said. "You know how I earn my living. I'm a thief."

"But, Mouse," I said, "this is my room."

"Well, I'm sorry," he answered. "How should I know that?"

I said, "I don't see how you could help but know it, with all these pictures of me all over the walls."

"Look, Tootchoo," he said. "What do you think I do when I'm robbing people—look at pictures?"

He was so mad it took me twenty minutes to make up with him. Well, anyway, I made him a drink and we sat down to talk about old times while he took our stuff out of the sack. Gracie came in with her arms full of bundles and joined us.

After Mouse left, Gracie said, "Nat, darling, one of the things I love about being married to you is meeting your wonderful friends."

We had a fine trip over. The only trouble was, everyone dressed for dinner at night, and the woman never wore the same evening dress twice. Gracie only had two, but that didn't bother us. Fortunately the *Leviathan* was so big that it had several dining rooms. We figured that with a different audience, lack of wardrobe wouldn't matter; so instead of changing clothes, we changed rooms every night.

Speaking of wardrobe, I had supplied myself carefully before we left New York. I wasn't going to have the English think I didn't know how to dress. While in England, do as the English do, I had told myself. Now the only Englishmen I had ever known were a dancing act, and I remembered exactly how they were attired. I duplicated the outfit, and the day we arrived in London we checked into a little hotel on Half Moon Street, and I dressed to go see my agent, Henry Shereck. I wore morning coat, striped pants, chamois gloves, hat turned up on one side, down on the other, spats, and a cane with a gold handle. I was no dope—I didn't want to be conspicuous and have everybody think I was a tourist.

I was so taken with myself that I forgot about traffic going the opposite way in England. Being an American, I looked the American way; and being English, the traffic was going the English way. I caught my cane in the spokes of the wheel of a passing cab. It flipped out of my hand and I never stopped to look for it. I was so embarrassed I kept right on walking.

I arrived at my agent's in a state of shock. Shereck looked up from his work and said, "*Who* are you?"

I said, "George Burns of Burns and Allen."

I Love Her, That's Why!

Shereck stopped his work and said, "I'm sure Val Parnell would like to see you." Parnell was the booker for the Victoria Palace. Shereck took me to him and introduced me.

Parnell just stared at me in my morning coat, striped pants, turned-down hat and my chamois gloves. He said, "Young man, you're dressed a little too early. This is Friday and you don't open until Monday."

I got back to the hotel and out of the clothes as soon as possible. This was tough, as I couldn't get my hand out of my sleeve because I was still clutching the gold knob of my cane. (The editors say this last line sounds contrived, and they happen to be right.) I didn't know until later that after I left, Parnell and Shereck died laughing. Parnell said, "If that's the way Burns dresses on the street we've got to get him on a golf course." They invited me to play. I accepted, and I arrived dressed in dark-gray pants and dark-blue coat—I'd learned my lesson. There were Shereck and Parnell, both of them huge men, dressed in plus fours, with socks that had tassels on them. I looked at them and said, "Gentlemen, you don't open until Monday." You see, you never know.

As we played golf, the thought remained in the back of my mind that we had one open week out of our five still to fill in. Parnell couldn't hit his hat. I complimented him on his game but managed to correct him at the same time. I'd say, "That's strange, that shot should have been good—you follow through so well." He hadn't followed through at all, but the next time he did. I kept complimenting and correcting and telling him he was great, and

132

pretty soon he began hitting the ball. When I thought he was in a good mood I said, "Mr. Parnell, the week of the fourteenth we have open, and if you could possibly book us into the Shepherd's Bush Empire that week I'd sure appreciate it."

He looked at me. "Burns," he said, "do you really think I'm a great golfer or are you trying to fill in that week?"

I said, "I think you are a great golfer, but I certainly want that week."

Parnell said, "Tell you what—if I hit my next drive over two hundred yards and stay on the fairway, the week of the fourteenth is booked." He stepped up to the ball, and it looked as if Ben Hogan hit the shot for him. He split the fairway in half for about two hundred and fifty yards right down the middle. He turned to me and said, "Burns, the week of the fourteenth you play Shepherd's Bush."

I said, "Mr. Parnell, now I can really tell you the truth. You're the lousiest golfer I've ever played with."

Monday we opened at the Victoria Palace. The people backstage were wonderful. They even asked us where we wanted to be on the bill. We went on after the "Victoria Girls," who were a sort of a chorus. We had an encore we used in case we were a hit. I would come out and say, "Ladies and gentlemen, we would like to do a little more, but we're not prepared." Then Gracie would interrupt and say, "*I* am." Then she would talk, and then I would talk, until we were both talking competitively, and it would end with one of our big jokes.

Opening night, we were a hit and we were doing

133

this encore. I said, "Ladies and gentlemen, we would like to do a little more, but we're not prepared." Gracie said, "*I* am." She talked, I talked, we were both talking, and suddenly an English gentleman in white tie and tails who was sitting in the 6th row, and who apparently didn't understand it was part of the act, rose to his feet, snapped his fingers, and said, "See here, let the little lady carry on." I looked at him. "I'll let her carry on," I said. But I forgot the act. He scared me to death.

We loved every bit of England, and returned once a year for five years to play there, and in Scotland and Ireland intermittently, on our Keith's commitments.

Gracie worked harder off stage than on. She had to see everything, and consequently so did I: the changing of the guard, all the castles, the Tower of London, etc., etc., etc.

The first time we played Glasgow we were a little nervous for fear the people wouldn't understand us. Instead, we didn't understand them. They all sounded as if they were doing syncopated patter.

Scotland was a nation of Harry Lauders to us. At the Empire Theater, where we played in Glasgow, they had a trick that was brand new to us. The Thursday matinee, the theatrical profession was allowed in free. The little acts around Scotland would come with paper and pencil and take down your jokes and when you left the country they would use them. After our opening routine I looked out at this scribbling audience and said, "Just tell me if I'm going too fast for you and I'll slow down."

One year while we were in England, we were asked to replace Fred and Adele Astaire in "Funnyface," but we were unable to because we had to return to New York to play the Palace. We were now doing a mixture of "Dizzy," "Lambchops," and "Sixty-Forty," and had started the jokes about Gracie's family—her brother, in particular, which later gave us our greatest publicity boost.

The day before we opened at the Palace we ran into Joe Frisco, who told us a wonderful joke he said we could use. It's an old joke now, but it wasn't then. We tried out the joke the opening matinee and it got a great laugh. The routine went like this:

GRACIE: My brother used to love to go out hunting. He used to take out four dogs and go out hunting, then he'd come back, and the next day he'd take out four more dogs and go out hunting. Then the next day—

GEORGE: Wait a minute—wait a minute. What did he do with the dogs he took out yesterday?

GRACIE: He shot those.

GEORGE: He'd take out dogs and shoot them?

GRACIE: Accidentally. He used to aim at the birds.

GEORGE: But he'd shoot the dogs.

GRACIE: Boom!

GEORGE: A dead dog.

GRACIE: Yeah.

GEORGE: What birds did he go out hunting for?

GRACIE: Heppelwhites.

GEORGE: Heppelwhites? That must be a bird that came out this season.

GRACIE: No, the heppelwhite is a bird that flies backward.

GEORGE: Flies backward?

GRACIE: Yes. He's not interested in where he's going. He's only interested in where he's been.

GEORGE: Your brother sounds like a great shot. Why don't you go out with him sometime?

GRACIE: I did. I went out duck hunting with him once. I used to hold onto the ducks while he'd shoot them.

GEORGE: You held onto the ducks while he shot them? What would happen if he missed the ducks and shot you?

GRACIE: Then the ducks had hold of me.

GEORGE: This family of yours—did you all live together?

GRACIE: Yes. My father, my uncle, my cousin, my brother, and my nephew used to sleep in one bed, and my—

GEORGE: I'm surprised your grandfather didn't sleep with them.

GRACIE: He did. But he died, and they made him get up.

The same night we received a wire from Fred Allen asking us to take the joke about the bird flying backward out of the routine. It was his joke. Now you get used to an extra laugh, and if you take it out it leaves a hole big enough for a quartette to fall through.

I called Fred Allen and offered to buy it. I was willing to pay up to five hundred dollars for the joke, that's how much it was worth to us. But Fred wouldn't sell—he was in love with it, too.

At that time I was buying loose jokes from John P. Medbury. I called him in California and said, "I'm in a terrible spot. I've got to replace an important joke."

Medbury said, "What's the joke?"

I said, "It's about a bird that flies backward— it's not interested in where it's going, it's interested in where it's been."

Without hesitating a minute he said, "Have the bird fly upside down, so if you shoot it, it falls up." Quite a writer, Medbury.

During our various trips to England we went on radio for the BBC, still doing bits and pieces of "Dizzy," "Lambchops," "Sixty-Forty," and anything else I thought of. This was our first radio experience, and I was grateful for it because I recognized then that, if we were ever given a chance at it back home, radio was a good medium for us.

We got the chance, but we took a crack at another medium first.

The day after we arrived home from one of our trips abroad we made our first motion picture.

15

MY MOTHER missed our first performance at the Palace because she was too ill to be moved. She was too ill to be moved the second time too, but that didn't stop her. She had been bedridden in her home in Brooklyn for a year with a heart condition brought on by lobar pneumonia. Her behavior as a patient would have made you believe she was up and everybody else was down. She ran the house from her bed, and everybody in it ragged. No manager ever did a better job of organizing a show.

Her main ambition was to get rid of the practical nurse we had hired to care for her. She was always sending her on unnecessary errands just to get her out of the way. The nurse tried to kid her about her condition, and it annoyed Mamma. She was seriously ill and she knew it, so what was the point of all the phony cheerfulness and "You'll be up and around in no time" dialogue?

My sister Goldie didn't come off any better in trying to kid her than the nurse. Gracie and I were on

138

the road, and Mamma looked forward to our letters. When she didn't get one in the mail, she showed her disappointment. One day when she was feeling real bad, and there wasn't any letter, Goldie tried to cheer her up by inventing one. She said, "Here's a nice letter from Nat, Mamma. It says, 'Dear Mamma: Hope you are feeling better. We are a smash in Tacoma—in fact, we went over so great that now they've got us opening the show.' "

"Hold it, Goldie, hold it," Mamma said. "What are you trying to make up? That's not a letter from Nat. They're not opening a show—that's for acrobats." Goldie tried to stammer her way out of this, but Mamma stopped her by saying, "Now, Goldie, why don't you and the nurse take a nice little walk?"

Soon after this, she had a very bad attack and we were all sent for. She was glad to see us, but worried at our all having come from so far. Gracie and I were playing Seattle at the time.

"Look," she said, "you are here because you think I am dying. I am not dying. I am not dying because I am not ready yet. When I am ready I will let you know. Now you should all go back to your business. I'll be up to see Nat and Gracie play the Palace—I missed the first time, but I won't miss the second." And she didn't.

Eight months later I hired a car, and my brother Willie and I wrapped her in blankets and drove her from Brooklyn to the Palace. We had an aisle seat for her, and brought her into the theater just at the intermission. I left her with Willie and went backstage. There was another act first, then us, then

Elsie Janis, who was headliner. We were a riot—
never had such an audience. They called us back
time after time, and Gracie and I were thrilled that
Mamma was seeing us under the greatest circum-
stances in show business. It was perfect. After the
show we drove Mamma back to Brooklyn, and on the
way I said, "Well, Mamma, who was the best on that
bill?" She said, "Elsie Janis."

Mamma always prayed for all of her children, but
asked only one favor for herself. She wanted to die
in her right mind and with her children around her.
She was granted almost all of her wish. Most of her
children were with her, and she was definitely in her
right mind. My brother Willie was still living at
home, and spent a lot of time with Mamma.

One night Mamma pointed to a copy of Dreiser's
An American Tragedy on her bedside table. Willie
had been reading it to her for several weeks. "We'd
better hurry up with this book," she said. "Maybe
you should read a little faster or skip the dull parts,
otherwise I'll come to the end before you do."

Willie called the doctor the next day. The doctor
told Willie that this looked like it. He told Mamma
she was going to be fine. She just gave him that look
and said, "Doctor, we know, don't we? So what's the
use of kidding? Why get the children's hope up? This
is nothing sad. I don't want any crying. Crying is
for misery. I said I'd tell you when I was ready . . .
well, I'm ready. My children are good, they are in **no**
trouble, and I am going to meet Papa. I am a happy
woman."

That night Willie took her hand, and it **was**

140

frighteningly cold. He held her up and gave her some digitalis, which was her emergency heart medicine. He sent the nurse to call the doctor, and brought some hot tea. Mamma took the medicine; then she said, "Willie, you are a good boy. I'll take the medicine and the tea—I'll even throw in a little aspirin. But you're wasting valuable time. There is so much to be done. First, have the nurse clean the house. There will be people here for the funeral, and I wouldn't want they should think the Birnbaums don't keep a good house. You should be able to eat off the floor. Now shut the door."

Willie shut the door, and Mamma said, "Reach under my pillow. You will find two one-hundred-dollar bills. One is for you, one for Sammy. The other children are working, but you and Sammy are not. This will give you both a start. Not a big start, but a start. Now when you wire Nat and Gracie about the funeral, don't do it until after their last performance."

She then proceeded to give complete instructions for her funeral. In the orthodox Jewish religion there is a ceremony connected with funerals which is called Shiva. It is a period of seven days' mourning in which the male children are supposed to go in stocking feet, cover their heads, and tear their clothes as a token of grief. Mamma was deeply religious, but she changed a few of the rules.

"I don't want any crying," she said. "This is an order. I do not want any clothes torn—who knows? this may be your only suit—or if it makes you feel better, wear something you don't care about. You and Sammy and the rest of the children should sit Shiva seven days, but Nat has a show to do, and he isn't too religious anyway, so he doesn't have to. You could tell him, though, it wouldn't hurt him to pray a couple of days. Be sure to pay the nurse tonight. You won't need her tomorrow. Finally, this is very important: tomorrow have lots of hot coffee. When Uncle Frank comes to the funeral and there's no hot coffee, you know what a terrible fuss he'll make. Now please, push my bed over to the window and pull up the shade."

Willie moved the bed to the window; and when he had pulled up the shade, Mamma administered the last rites to herself according to her faith, and, having made her peace with God, kept her date with my father.

The minute I got the wire from the family I started to prepare Gracie for the funeral. I said, "Gracie, you must know ahead of time what this is going to be like. Nobody in the world cries like my family. Anyway, they cry easy and this time they've got something to cry about. Don't forget we're seven sisters and five brothers and dozens of nieces and nephews and when we all cry together—that's crying. You've never heard anything like it. I just want you to know what you're getting into."

But I was wrong. As far as the funeral was concerned, just the way Mamma set it up, that's the way we had it. No crying, and plenty of hot coffee for Uncle Frank. Only two things were different. Gracie, not having got her instructions from headquarters, cried, and I prayed for the full week.

The $1,700 Disappointment Act

16

THE night the *Berengaria* docked in New York we were invited to a party. At the party Arthur Lyons came over to me and said, "How would you like to make a nine-minute short for Warner Brothers in Astoria tomorrow morning? Fred Allen was supposed to do it, but he's sick. You can pick up seventeen hundred dollars." I'd never heard of $1,700 in my life, especially for nine minutes' work, and immediately said yes. Fred Allen's cold made us a $1,700 disappointment act.

When we arrived in Astoria at 8:30 in the morning to shoot, we found that we were supposed to work in a living-room set. This would have been all right, except I had to rewrite a lot of dialogue which would make it reasonable for me to be wearing a hat. You see, our trunks weren't off the dock yet, and my toupee was in my trunk.

The first person I saw on the set was a man named Murry Roth, who was a childhood school friend of

143

mine. I said, "For heaven's sake, Murry, what are you doing here?"

He said, "I'm in show business."

I said, "You're in show business! For what? You can't act, you can't sing, you can't dance, you can't skate."

"George," he said, "I'm a director. I'm directing you in this picture."

I said, "You're kidding! I don't believe it."

"You don't, eh?" he said. "Watch this." He yelled, "Lights!" They went on. He yelled, "Off!" They went off. "See?" he said.

We had to improvise an act because of my not being able to take off my hat. Gracie came on the set, looked in boxes, behind curtains, etc. I said, "What are you looking for?" She said, "The audience." I said, "Look into the lens of that camera— that's your audience. Well, Gracie, let's see now —how's your brother?" And she told me for nine minutes. At the end of that time I looked at my watch. I said, "That's all—our nine minutes are up, we just made seventeen hundred dollars. Gracie, say good-by." She said, "Good-by." I said, "Wave to the lens." She waved to the lens, and we went to the bank.

That was our first motion-picture experience, and just between us, the picture was not the greatest. But we were happy, and our agent, Arthur Lyons, was happy. The Warner Brothers were not.

I couldn't get that $1,700 for nine minutes out of my head and wanted to make more shorts. So I wrote one called, "I Want to Buy a Tie." I gave it to Lester

144

Hammel of the Morris Agency and he came up with an offer from Paramount of $1,000 for it. That old second-encore feeling came over me and I said we would sell it only if we could play it, and for an additional $250. I wasn't afraid to face a camera; the trunks were off the dock and I could work without a hat.

Paramount bought the short. It was a smash. They signed us for another at $2,500, then for one at $3,000, then $4,000. We were finally making four a year for Paramount.

We were happy.

Our agent was happy.

The Warner Brothers were still unhappy.

A year later we were up to our necks in radio.

17

ONE week later we were booked into the Palace again, still doing "Lambchops," and we were a hit. Arthur Willy, who was then the booker for the Palace, said he would keep us on another week if we would change the act and Gracie would be mistress of ceremonies. I turned him down immediately. Change the act! And at the Palace yet! In those days if we changed two lines, we booked Altoona or Scranton to break them in.

The same night I ran into George Jessel at Sardi's. I told him about turning down the offer from Willy. He listened to me and then said, "Excuse me a minute, I have to make a phone call." When he came back he said, "I just called Willy and told him you'd changed your mind about playing the second week, and accepted it for you." When I got through sputtering, he said, "Don't be silly, George, the Palace audiences are the kindest in the world. They'll understand if you're not your greatest. They'll love you for trying. After all, you have made fourteen shorts; you can use some of that material. You're much too good to be afraid. Wait and see, they'll accept you. I'll bet on it."

He was right. We went on and the audience was wonderful. We had a hit, and, thanks to Georgie, we've never been afraid of a new joke since.

In the development of this act we needed something to get off with. Because we couldn't think of anything new, I put back an old bit I'd taken out years before, when we were doing "Dizzy."

Toward the end of the act I'd say, "Music," and we would dance. I'd say, "Stop." Then we'd tell a joke. I'd say, "Music"—and this went on for several minutes and then we'd dance right off the stage. As I say, we had done this before, the first week we were together, and it fell flat on its face. We did it at the Palace and it was a smash. This was another sign of progress. The bit was just as good then, but *we* weren't.

Four months later we played the Palace again. Eddie Cantor and George Jessel were the headliners. The show stayed on for nine weeks, playing to capacity. Two weeks later the Palace closed—this bill practically locked the theater.

During the Palace date, Eddie Cantor called me and asked if Gracie could go on his Chase and Sanborn radio show. I said sure, if he would use four or five minutes of our material. He insisted on it. Eddie used the material and played straight for Gracie. He gave her everything, and she was a riot. Gracie did so well that the next week both of us were booked on the Rudy Vallee show, which was our first

American radio job together. The following week we went on the Guy Lombardo show. Then we stayed on a second week with Lombardo.

About ten days after our first performance, the sponsors of the show, Robert Burns Panatellas, received a letter from some college students. It was almost poetic. It said, in part, "For two years we have listened to the 'sweetest music this side of heaven,' the music of Guy Lombardo. In the frat house we could find the radio dial by the glow of a Robert Burns Panatella. Now this lovely music is interrupted by a succession of tired he-she jokes we could have gotten out of *College Humor* ourselves." It said more, too. And it had sixty signatures.

John Reber, who was head man at J. Walter Thompson's, the agency handling the show, showed me the letter and I thought we'd had it. I expected him to hand us our pictures. Instead he said, "George, when sixty people go to the trouble to tell you you're awful, you must have something." He kept us on. Seven weeks later we received another letter from the sixty students saying they'd gotten used to us; in fact, they liked us. That scared me again. I figured if they liked us maybe Reber didn't. But he did. We stayed with the Lombardos for two years. Then Guy went with another sponsor, and we took over the show.

Gracie was beginning to be so well known that she was recognized everywhere she went. One day the cook asked her to buy a rolling pin when she was out shopping. She came home looking a little shattered. "I had a strange experience in Bloomingdale's," she said. "I picked up a rolling pin off the counter and the salesgirl said, 'I suppose that's to hit George with?' Then she broke herself up over her own joke and pretty soon there was a big crowd around me laughing and asking this kind of question. I got so embarrassed I dropped the rolling pin and bought two end tables instead." They came in very handy because we didn't have a couch.

Part of our radio success during the time we were with Lombardo was due to a brilliant publicity stunt conceived by Bob Taplinger, who was head of publicity for CBS. He came to me with the idea, and we kicked it around until we came up with the plan that Gracie should be looking for a lost brother. She would start by talking about him on our show, have newspaper plants about him, and finally she would walk into other shows while they were on the air, looking for him. This was unheard of, it had not only never been done before, but everyone said we'd never get away with it. We not only got away with it, it got away with us.

We had no conception of how such an idea could pick up momentum. We hadn't reckoned with how much the newspaper reporters would love the whole project. They took it to their hearts as if they'd thought of it. Gracie was photographed everywhere looking for the brother: the top of the Empire State Building, at Coney Island, anywhere any one of them thought might be a funny place to shoot her.

In the first ten days of the campaign Gracie picked up a million dollars' worth of free publicity. She appeared everywhere in radio where she wouldn't be expected—in the middle of a daytime serial, a soap opera, a dramatic show where the hero was down in a submarine, a mystery, always asking if anyone had seen her brother. It broke people up and they spent hours switching dials around to catch her in some spot she had no business being. Then the public got in on the joke with the same enthusiasm as the newspapermen. Gracie started receiving letters with photographs, mostly of people's backs saying, "Is this your brother?" She also had some letters from people who thought they were.

In the middle of the campaign Rudy Vallee booked us on his NBC show to have Gracie continue her search for the brother. The powers at NBC said *no,* if she didn't find him on the NBC show she'd take the audience back to CBS while she looked for him. They said she could be on the show, but she could not mention her brother. The scripts were rewritten and the brother eliminated. Then we went on the air and Vallee picked up the wrong script. He mentioned the brother, and they took us off the air. This made the newspapermen furious. They flooded us with more publicity, and the campaign, which didn't need it, had a fresh start. The funny thing about all of this was that we had NBC to thank for fabulous CBS publicity.

At the end of ten days we stopped the campaign while it was still on the upswing, because we were afraid the public would tire of it. Everyone had had a wonderful time with Gracie's lost brother except Gracie's real brother, who just wanted to get lost, and at times Gracie, who got pretty tired of answering foolish questions.

After the success of the stunt everybody started to go on each other's programs, but we got the cream off the top. It taught us the value of publicity and we never forgot it. In the years that followed, the cooperation of the press was invaluable in the development of the character Gracie plays and in helping to familiarize the public with it. As a matter of fact, nine years later Gracie was running for President.

18

I JUST noticed that I've said a lot about Gracie on-stage but very little about Gracie off. If that is true, it is because talking about Gracie is very hard for me. Why? I love her, that's why. I can talk about a performance she gave, or a joke she told, or how pretty she looked, but to try to tell you what she is like, really like . . . I don't know. I'll try, but remember, I'm a comic, not a poet.

To begin with, I think she's the greatest: the best wife, the best mother, and the best sport—a real dead-on dame. Now I'd better explain about that best sport. She is a lady loaded with more problems than anyone I know, and I have never heard her beef. I told you before that she is a fine dramatic actress who, because she met me, has become a world-wide symbol of sweet absurdity. (How do you like that "symbol of sweet absurdity"?—don't forget I have a very high-class collaborator.) Gracie's character has had its artistic and financial rewards, but it has also taken its toll. It hasn't always been easy.

152

Mostly about Gracie—but Not Entirely

Most of my work is behind the scenes. When we work, particularly now that we are in television, the main burden of performance is on Gracie. If you look at the show, you will notice that she is on with an enormous amount of unnatural dialogue almost the entire time. As she is a complete perfectionist, she is always letter perfect, which means days of memorizing before we shoot. She just gets one show committed to memory, shoots it; and before she has a chance to take a deep breath, next week's script has arrived and she starts on that. On the set she gives absolutely no trouble and makes no demands. She arrives on time, does the job, jokes with the crew, and in general behaves less like a star than any actress I ever knew, particularly as when she shuts the dressing room door and goes home, she's through. The day's work is done and there is no further discussion about it. She figures there's no time for temperament when you're on every week.

Gracie has been named as one of the best-dressed women in the country. She was pleased by the honor; she loves clothes, and she tries to live up to the title. She got her training early, because when she was a little girl her mother used to make her beautiful clothes. When Gracie was going to "The Star of the Sea" School in San Francisco and dancing in the school plays, her mother made her costumes that no other mother could top—she wanted her always to look pretty.

Her father, who was the first minstrel man in San Francisco, was watching Mrs. Allen sew spangles on a costume one day and said, "You'll never get anywhere in show business with spangles on your skirt. You have to be a character." It's nice both her mother and father got their wish.

As Gracie never wears the same thing twice on the show, it means endless wardrobe conferences and fittings, which are extremely tiring. She also has interviews, which are an important part of our business but which are exhausting to Gracie, because most reporters expect something from her that she is not prepared to give. People who don't know her expect her to be funny. She is, extremely, but not in the professional Gracie way. She has an entirely individual humor, but it is only apparent when she is not under pressure. Now if the reporter is smart and asks her about the children or about me, he'll get a fabulous interview. She'll talk his ears off—about Sandy, Ronnie, me, Sandy's baby, Mousie the poodle, the house, clothes, gin rummy. She'll tell hilarious anecdotes, drag out photographs, and make him a cocktail. He'll leave the house completely charmed by her, chuckling over the great material he's picked up, go back to his typewriter, and find out that he's dead. There's just one thing she didn't mention: Gracie.

This modesty of hers is absolutely real. She honestly believes that she is not an interesting person. The fact that a lot of people think she is doesn't alter her opinion. She goes along with Jimmy Durante's "What is everybody's opinion compared to mine?"

For a woman who likes to be alone, Gracie has landed in a great spot—she never can be. If she shops, she is recognized, and people either expect her to tell jokes or they tell them to her. They ask if she's "really like that?" She always says, "Of course," and lets them play the part. The public really made the character anyway; it belongs to them, and she feels the obligation to go along with the gag. Going along with the gag, however, takes quite a lot of her time. She works so hard seven days a week that I know there are times when she's sick to death of it, but as I say, I have never heard a beef out of her.

Even in our social life I've got her working. She laughs up all my jokes, some of which she's heard for thirty years.

Now I'm a good husband and I always switch the finish for her, but with some wives that wouldn't help. Gracie laughs just as if each time was the first time, and she laughs not only at the nice jokes but at some that aren't so nice. Let's face it: sometimes I talk like I'm in mixed company, and sometimes like a refugee from a stag dinner. While I'm guilty of this Friars Club dialogue, Gracie never scolds or faints at my language. She just says, "Oh, George." That's all: "Oh, George." And if I'm in form, I'm good for about twenty or thirty "Oh, Georges" a night.

She is such a complete lady, and by nature so proper, that I know she has been honestly shocked by me. But I'll never hear it from her. She just continues to laugh in the right places, and then I think she goes to church and lights a candle for me. I can't think of any other reason why I've been so lucky dodging those lightning bolts.

Within this tiny woman, there is great courage

155

and character. She has had every known accident, including almost being burned to death as a child, with the result that she came close to losing her right arm. And she has been plagued for years with shattering migraine headaches, probably brought on by the chronic strain of making like someone she isn't. And yet she has never missed a performance. If there's one thing she hates, it's the outdoors. I love it. She likes to stay indoors, rest, read, or play gin with the girls. So when we get a few days off she insists on going to Palm Springs where the golf, tennis, and swimming are great, because she knows it's good for me.

My belief is that a lot of show-business marriages go on the rocks because the man and woman are in competition rather than in partnership. With us, it's very simple: Gracie takes the lead on-stage; I take it, off. We both have our own departments. She stays in hers, and I'm into everybody'. Gracie's has always been the greater acting talent; she is the star, but you'd never know it. She has always allowed me to advise her, direct her, and to speak for us.

One thing I don't do is think for her. She thinks for herself, and when she's made up her mind, that's it. Maybe she inherits her determination from her Aunt Clara, who wanted to marry a particularly wealthy man, so she threw herself under the feet of the horses that were pulling his carriage. The driver stopped the horses and this gentleman stepped out of the carriage, picked her up, and drove her home. Six months later Aunt Clara married him. She was sixteen and he was seventy-six, but very rich. He

156

lived twenty years. (This, incidentally, is a true story, as opposed to a few others I've told you.)

I think a lot of Gracie's determination is based on her size—she's only five feet tall. She felt when she was young that people took advantage of her because she was so little. Actually, what happened was that being pretty as well as little, people really want to take care of her instead of advantage of her. Except, of course, that man in the elevator once. He tried to get fresh with her, and she hit him over the head with her handbag. Gracie always has a good reason behind her determination except, I think, in the case of this book. She said people were only interested in the character she played, not in the real Gracie. I leave the answer up to you readers. I'm prejudiced.

To sum up my feeling about Gracie, I might say I have only one complaint: My wife understands me.

And now, enough about her. This is *my* biography. Where were we?

Anyway, things were going well. While we were still with the Lombardos we came to Hollywood and made a series of "Big Broadcast" pictures for Paramount, and one picture called "Many Happy Returns." Then we started a new radio show called "The Adventures of Gracie," and moved from the Edison Hotel to the Essex House.

One night we were standing in the living room, looking out of the big window at Central Park. It was beautiful—all dark and velvety with a sprinkling of lights. It looked like a very expensive backdrop. I felt great. Full of that full stomach, pretty home, five-year contract, we wowed 'em feeling. Everything was just too good. I put my arm around Gracie and said, "You know, Googie, if we never have more than this, we have more than anybody."

Gracie said, "Yes, we've got everything, except the most important thing."

I said, "What's that?"

She said, "Children."

This surprised me, because when we were first married, we both wanted children and Gracie was the one who said "No." As you know, we had no money, and were on the road all the time. Gracie thought it was unfair to children to drag them all over the country. I remember her words exactly: "I don't want a child I have to tie to a chair while we're on entertaining," she said. "I've seen too many of them, poor babies. I want a child when we can afford to give it a proper home." When that time came, it just never happened.

Now when she brought up the subject I didn't know exactly how to react, because I hadn't given it much thought. I knew Gracie had and that she had felt the need greatly, but because of this chronic good sportsmanship I have referred to, Gracie never complained about not being a mother. And along with the good sportsmanship went the quality of never compromising. Anything that was done had to be done the right way, including having children.

Children were no novelty to me; I'd been brought up with too many of them. Besides, I didn't know whether I'd be a good father. I was so interested in the latest variation on "Who was that lady I saw you with?" that I didn't know whether I could switch to "How did it go in school today?"

I wasn't against it, I wasn't for it; if she wanted it, O.K.

"Well, how do you want to go about it?" I asked.

"It's very simple," she said. "I want to adopt a baby."

Right then I knew I was about to become a father. "All right," I said. "When?"

"Tomorrow," she answered. Her decisions are always immediate, and this time even sooner.

She took the first train in the morning to Chicago and went to the Cradle. It seems she and Mrs. Florence Walwrath, the founder of the Cradle, had been having long-distance telephone conversations. Mrs. Walwrath is an absolutely wonderful woman who has made hundreds of children and parents happy with her adoption service. These two girls got along just great. Gracie, as usual, knew exactly what she wanted, and Mrs. Walwrath understood perfectly. Gracie wanted a girl—a girl named Sandy Burns. We had decided on the nickname first. Gracie had to have a Sandy. The Sandra was just an excuse for the nickname.

Mrs. Walwrath took all our particulars, and the red tape started to unfold. I think Gracie was terribly disappointed—she didn't know it would all take so long. Instead of going home with a baby, she was told to go home and they would call her in a few months: "Don't call us; we'll call you."

The next four months were the most hectic of our lives. Gracie worked herself to death being a mother

159

before she was one. She bought toys, furniture, and enough little clothes to outfit Singer's Midgets for a two-year run. Every time the phone rang she jumped for it faster than she ever had when we were hungry and waiting for a call from our agent. One night she picked up the phone. The operator said Chicago was calling. Gracie screamed, "George!"

I ran in from the other room, took a look at her face, and thought there was a death in the family. I said, "What's the matter?"

She put her hand over the mouthpiece and said, "It's only the Morris office. They want to know if we'll do an auto show for fifteen thousand dollars." Now we were a parental disappointment act.

Then she hired this horse—or rather this nurse; she looked like a horse. We were both scared to death of her and she knew it. She also knew how anxious Gracie was to have everything perfect for the baby, and she took outrageous advantage of us because of it. She was stage-managing the show weeks before the baby arrived.

Then one day the right Chicago call came through, and Mrs. Walwrath said, "Come and get your baby!"

Gracie flew out of there faster than Owen Mc-Giviney, the quick-change artist, could take off his hat. She picked up Mary Kelly, and they were off to Chicago. The minute they were gone, I called about twenty of our friends and invited them to a home-coming party for Sandy, and I can tell you now, the Palace never made me as nervous as staging this show. The nurse didn't approve, but that didn't stop me; she wasn't invited.

160

When the girls arrived at the Cradle, Mrs. Walwrath brought out a baby all wrapped up in a blanket and handed it to Gracie. Gracie took the baby in her arms and looked down at it. The baby just didn't look like Gracie expected Sandy to look. Gracie didn't say anything, but Mrs. Walwrath, that wonderful woman, sensed it.

"Heavens!" she said, "I think we've picked the wrong baby for you—I'd forgotten how tiny you were. We always like to have the babies as much like the parents as possible. Let me show you our little five-week-old girl—she's one of the smallest babies we've ever had."

They brought out the other baby. Gracie took one look and said, "That's Sandy."

It was a good thing they made such an effort to match the small baby with the small parent. Sandy is now five feet eight.

The three girls arrived after a nerve-racking trip. Gracie and Mary had been afraid to sleep for fear something would happen to the baby. Then they dozed off, and Gracie's fur coat fell on the baby's basket. They were sure it might have smothered her, and they were so frightened that something else might happen that they sat up all night. Gracie was white. The only thing she was more afraid of than the nurse was the baby.

This party was the best sociable I've ever been to. Here we were with all our friends: Jack and Mary Benny, Blossom Seely and Benny Fields, Tom Fitzpatrick, Jesse Block and Eva Sully, Abe and Frances Lastfogel, Lou Holtz, Jack and Flo Haley, Orry

I Love Her, That's Why!

Kelly, Jane and Goodie Ace, and more—all of them show people. And in that large group of people, not one of them had a baby. Ours was the first. The way they acted, you'd have thought they never saw one, let alone had one. I, of course, took one look, and it was the same as with Gracie—this was Sandy. She looked up at me with that steady, no-nonsense look she never outgrew, and I thought, now I've got two of them; this is another real dead-on dame.

Gracie let me take the baby around to show her off. I showed her off right. They got to see her in the proper order, according to their billing at the time. Blossom Seely was first; she was headlining the Palace that week. Jack Benny was second; he was next to closing at the Riverside. When I pulled back the blanket for him to look he said, "Oh, my God, how can anything be so small?" Yesterday he went to see Sandy's baby daughter and he said, "Oh, my God, how can anything be so small?" In twenty years no new material. His success must be due to his delivery.

Anyway, we were having the time of our lives and so was Sandy. Even at five weeks she was very poised. Everybody was talking and cooing and upstaging each other in front of Sandy's basket, when there was the loudest *shhhhhhhh!* you ever heard, and that cop-nurse came in, took the baby away, and told us we would have to be quiet. But the party went on in whispers. It seems everybody was reminded of a baby story.

We were a sensation in our crowd from then on. We did matinees with the bath routine. Friends took

162

to dropping in to watch this act. I allowed them in billing order, as before. Poor Larry Reilly was the last one to see Sandy take her bath—he was laying off. We had a real run with this baby monopoly, and then the Bennys spoiled everything by getting Joanie. This competition affected business for a while, but it didn't change our point of view that this was the only baby that existed. In fact, we were so in love with her that it scared us. She was only the greatest—the most beautiful, the cutest, and everything you would order, if that's the way it worked.

One night we were looking out the window at the park. I had Sandy in my arms. I turned to Gracie and said, "Well, Googie, now we *do* have everything."

"Everything except a boy," she said, and kept looking out the window.

"When?" I said, as if I didn't know.

Five minutes later, she put in that Chicago call again.

When we got word the baby was due, we moved to a triplex in the Lombardy on which we had to take a two-year lease. Here we had space upstairs for the kids not to be disturbed. Gracie bought more stuff, this time for a boy. She bought everything except a tuxedo for him. We bought a car so the kids could be driven to the park, and hired a chauffeur, because we couldn't drive. We also hired a cook, because up to now we had always eaten in restaurants.

We had a harder time deciding on a name this time. I wanted to call him Allen Burns, after both

163

of us, but Gracie said that was too theatrical. Then she said, "Of course, my favorite nickname for a boy is Ronnie." Our son's name is Ronald.

We didn't have as long a wait this time; the baby was premature. I was upset when Gracie arrived with Ronnie. She held him out to me and said, "Nat, I took one look at him and fell in love with his eyes. He's not well, but we can make him well." This was something I hadn't bargained for. I saw what she meant about the eyes. They were enormous, dark, and sad, in a tiny, pinched white face. I said, "Gracie, wait a minute—I don't mind a responsibility, but I do mind a sickly one." Gracie said, "That's the same chance we would have taken if we'd had him. Nat, look at those eyes." I did. She was right.

After Sandy's roly-poly first year, Ronnie was a hard baby to care for at first. He was a real sick little guy. He couldn't be bathed except in oil, he had to be wrapped in cotton all the time, and he didn't gain enough. Actually it took him about seven years to catch up with himself, physically. Now, we're afraid he'll never stop. The small white face is now brown from endless hours on a surfboard, there is a great deal of muscle involved, he's six feet one and still growing, and I imagine he has to beat the girls off with a stick.

We thought, when the kids were little, there never was and never could be anything like them. And then twenty years later, Sandy had Laurie.

I hate to brag, but we're one up on the group again. Ours is the first grandchild.

164

Guess What! Mamma Can Sew!

19

I DIDN'T mind any part of this new high-class living: triplex, nurse, cook, car—but the chauffeur . . . him I minded. He was hired to drive the children to the park. He drove the children to the park and me crazy. He took his job seriously, this man; had an answer for everything; and was equipped for any emergency. One night when he was driving us, Gracie said to me, "I have a hole in my stocking." He handed her a needle and thread. Neither rain nor snow nor sleet nor storm halted him in the pursuit of his duties. In fact, they encouraged him.

When I went to the Friars Club I used to have him stop a block away, and I'd walk—I wasn't about to have any of the members catch me with this chauffeur. That's all I'd need. I'd try to rush out of the car, but if the weather looked bad he'd park the car and run after me with an umbrella. I finally told him if he ever dared open the car door for me one more time he'd be fired. One day Jack Benny and I got out of the car and as we did Jack said, "Let's stop and get some cigars." Half a block later I looked in back of us and there was the chauffeur with a humidor of cigars in his hand. Benny screamed laughing. He said, "George, this is one of the funniest gags you've ever pulled on me." Being an honest man, I took a few bows.

Do you know, we had to move to California to get rid of that man?

Actually, we had to move to California to make a picture, but the offer couldn't have come at a better time. It gave me an excuse to fire the chauffeur.

That triplex turned out to be pretty expensive. We had taken it on a two-year lease, and were in it three months when we moved to Hollywood, and have been in Hollywood ever since. Anyway, the apartment was a nice place for our friends to stay when they were in New York.

Gracie had called her sister Bessie in California to get us a house. She got us a house: it was as big as Madison Square Garden. The dining room seated forty people—you couldn't invite less because the acoustics were so bad and the seats so far apart that you couldn't hear anybody. The house had so many rooms that we kept getting lost in it. For a guy who grew up in three rooms with eleven brothers and sisters, it was hard for me to relax in forty rooms with just my wife and two babies. The servants, of course, had separate quarters. There also were gardens and gardeners, and a swimming pool with a bridge over it, and a stable yet. Jack Benny came over to see the place and said, "What's with the stable?" I said, "Would I live in a house without a stable?" I hadn't been near a stable since I dressed with the man who handled Fink's mules when we were playing the Oriental in Chicago.

One night, when we'd been living there about nine months, I had some of the boys over for bridge—I think it was Al Jolson, George Levee, and George Jessel. We looked around for a place small enough to sit down and play cards in, and finally I said, "Let's go upstairs—there's a little room there we never use." We moved the table into the room and Jessel said, "Where can I hang my coat?" I pointed to a door and said, "Put it in there." He opened the door and there were five more rooms I didn't know we had.

After we moved out of the house because we all had colds all the time from the drafts in the halls, we bought our house on Maple Drive in Beverly Hills, where we still live. Arthur Lyons rented the old house, and after a few months we were invited to a party there. When we arrived I couldn't have been more surprised when the butler said, "The party is downstairs in the playroom."

"Playroom!" I said. When we got downstairs, I said to Arthur, "Do you know we lived in this house for one whole year, and I didn't know until tonight there was a playroom here."

Arthur said, "No kidding! You must be pretty un-observant."

I said, "I guess I am—it took me nine months to find out about the five rooms off that little sewing room upstairs."

"*Five rooms!*" he said.

167

I Love Her, That's Why!

Gracie took both houses in her stride, hired a butler, cook, and nurse, told them what our habits were, kept in her department and let them run theirs. This worked out in all cases except with the nurse: she was another beaut—old, like the New York one, and just as disagreeable. The only thing she liked less than children was actors. The minute one of our friends was in the middle of a story, she would somehow manage to make an entrance that killed the point. I must say she had perfect timing.

When we made the move to the other house Gracie said, "This is a good time to change nurses and get one that is young, loves children, and has a sense of humor." We got her. She was not only young, loved children, and had a sense of humor, she also had a son. That was the deal: if you got the nurse, you got the son. We signed. It was a good thing we did. Rose was wonderful, and so was Donald, her son. They were with us seven years, and Donald was the love of Sandy's life.

One night we were standing by the window looking out at the garden. It was beautiful. The roses were in bloom, so was the jasmine, and the orange tree was covered with blossoms—and oranges, too; they do that in California. All it lacked was a dancing act like Adelaide and Hughes who worked in full stage and that's what the yard looked like—ready for their entrance. Gracie put her arm through mine and said, "Now, Nat, we *do* have everything."

"Everything," I said, "except a swimming pool."

"If ever a family needed a swimming pool," said Gracie, "we're that family. The children are one and

168

two, I wouldn't go in the water if you gave me an Academy Award, and you can only do the slap-overhand." She was referring to the fact that I learned to swim in the East River. The slap was to push the garbage out of the way so you could proceed with the next stroke. I must have looked hurt at her reference to my style, because the next minute she said, "But for heaven's sake, Nat, if you want it, why not? We can afford it; and later, it will be wonderful for the children. . . . When do you want to start?"

I said, "I hired the men yesterday."

When the pool was completed, we bought little cork coats for the children and they paddled around in the pool. When she was four, Sandy, who had been taking swimming lessons, was allowed to take off the coat and swim without it. This insulted Ronnie, who insisted on taking off his too. Gracie tried to reason with him, but he persisted, so I said, "All right, he's got to be taught a lesson. Let him take it off. He'll sink, it will scare him, and he'll never do it again."

I stood by to rescue him as he jumped off the edge of the pool, swam over to the edge, got out, jumped in again, and swam over to the edge again. He kept this up for an hour. He certainly learned his lesson. Two years later he saved me from drowning.

As the kids became better and better swimmers, Gracie began to worry about what they would think of her not being able to swim at all. Now she was always much more concerned with the kids' opinion of her than anybody else's, so she had a little talk with the swimming teacher. She took eight lessons in all.

169

At the end of the eighth, she called the children out to the pool, said, "Watch this," dived off the board, swam the full length of the pool, got out, and has never been in since. That was sixteen years ago.

As the kids grew, Gracie and I found it increasingly hard to discipline them. Sandy invariably took the brunt of things, and always protected Ronnie. Ronnie, on the other hand, made it almost impossible to punish him, because he always beat you to the punch. If you punished him, he told you how to do it, after first telling you what an awful boy he'd been for doing something so terrible. By the time he got through with this "shame on me" routine, and had suggested that you send him to bed for the day, you were dead. There was nothing left to say. I spent all his early life wanting to say, "Get off my side so I can wallop you." Quite an operator, this one.

In one of my self-improvement periods I bought a forty-dollar dictionary, and you can see by this book that it was a worthwhile investment. Anyway, I came home one day to be faced by Gracie who said, "You'd better come see what's happened to the dictionary." I went into the library—well, we *call* it the library—and there were the two children and there was the dictionary, except for the pictures from the dictionary, which were in a neatly cut out pile on the floor.

Now, I'll say one thing for my role as a father. There were times when I knew exactly what to do. This was one of them. Gracie was going about it the wrong way. She was saying to Sandra, "What does Mesopotamia mean?" Both kids looked at her. Sandra said, "I don't know." Gracie said to Ronnie, "Do you know what it means?" Ronnie said, "No." Gracie said, "Ah, but the dictionary does know, and now you'll never know because you've cut it out."

"Just a minute," I said, "I'll take care of this. Sandra," I said, "did you do it?" She said, "No." "Ronnie," I said, "did you do it?" Ronnie said, "No." I said, "Ronnie, leave the room." When he left I said, "Sandra, I know you didn't do it, but where are the scissors Ronnie used?" Sandy said, "I don't know." I sent her out and sent for Ronnie. "Ronnie," I said, "I know you didn't do it, but where are the scissors Sandra used?" Ronnie said, "In the desk drawer." I said, "Ronnie, I'm sorry, I have to spank you, you have just given yourself away."

For sixteen years I've told this story, taking bows on my strategy. The other night Sandy said, "Daddy, I wish you'd stop telling that story about how clever you were in trapping Ronnie. I did it."

All of the kids' friends were the children of show people, and none of them were ever impressed by how big a star their mother or father was; the only thing that fazed them was when somebody wasn't. Sandy came home from school one day, thrilled to death, and said, "What do you think happened in school today? I met a girl and her father is in the felt-hat business!"

The children liked us fine, but were unimpressed with our talents, Gracie's or mine. The nurse listened to our weekly show, and she made them keep still so they had to listen to it too, but it was everyday stuff. One day Ronnie was running by Gracie in the hall, and she said, "Where are you going so fast?" He said, "I'm going over to Freddy Astaire's house, and I lost a button—I'm going to get Rose to fix it." Gracie said, "Whoa, wait a minute, I'll fix it." While she sewed it on, he stared at her as if he'd never seen her before, and when the Astaires' car came for him, he ran out the front door screaming, "Freddy—guess what! Mamma can sew!"

It's a funny thing about Hollywood children— very few of them want to follow in their parents' footsteps. I guess they see too early how hard it is. Also, curiously enough, it is not a business you can hand down to your son, like real estate, automobiles, or grocery stores. You can encourage him, tell him what you know about your craft, advise him, and finance him while he gets experience; but that's all. He must have that certain feel for it, and when his time comes to prove himself, it's the public which will decide whether he is to make his living this way. It may decide to "give him his pictures" and put him in another line of work. And there's no use arguing about it; the public, being the customer, is always right. The public was right in our case, and taught us a lesson we never forgot. We came to a point where we stopped making pictures because Gracie wanted to spend more time with the children. "I feel cheated," she said. "I want to see them grow." When she did both pictures and radio there just wasn't enough time at home, so we concentrated on radio.

Having decided to limit ourselves to radio, we were pretty shocked when our rating began to show a steady decline. Now, when you have a sudden drop in your rating of, say, eight or nine points, you don't worry: it means the President made a speech, or a new show came on, or something like that. But a gradual decline in points—that's murder. It means there's something the matter with your show. They don't like you. I went to all my friends and asked them what they thought was the trouble.

Benny said, "I think you're doing too many double routines." Cantor said, "I don't think you're doing enough double routines." Jessel said, "Gracie laughs too much." Holtz said, "Gracie doesn't laugh enough." Somebody said, "Try an eight-ball mike— it may sound better." Somebody else said, "It's the eight-ball mike; makes you sound muffled." Somebody said, "Wear high shoes." Somebody else said, "Wear low shoes." Well, with all this good advice, I finally got the answer myself.

We were too old for the he-she kind of jokes we were doing at the time. The character Gracie plays was flirting with the announcer, and we were having boy-friend, girl-friend jokes and insulting each other. Now you can insult your girl, but not your wife. Everybody knew we were married, and everybody knew we had growing children. The situation just wasn't true, and you have to have truth in a joke just the way you do in anything else, to make it any good. If it's basically dishonest, it isn't funny.

Our contracts were up, and were not renewed. The Morris office called and said we had an offer from Swan Soap for $7,500 a week for the package: that means the price includes everything—musicians, writers, director, and actors. It was much less than we had been getting.

"Is that the best deal you can get?" I said.

"It's the only deal," they answered.

"Take it," I said.

Now out of that $7,500 I paid my writers $3,500 a week. I never spent money better. I figured with the right words we could get our rating and our money back. I was right. We changed our entire basis of humor to a domestic-situation comedy, which is what we have today. Business seems to be good; and if there is a moral to this story, it is that if you're telling jokes for a living, see that they're no younger than you are.

Which brings me to the fact that the public, being the customer and always right, also, like mother, always knows best. It had the sense to know a good candidate when it saw one and got right behind Gracie when she ran for President of the United States.

Gracie's candidacy was based on the fact that my writers and I felt it was time we figured out something for Gracie to do with her spare time. I already explained to you how much of it she has: about an hour a week. Well, as long as she had it, we figured we'd use it. It was hard to think up something new for her. We had her chasing all over the country after her lost brother; playing her "Concerto for Index Finger" in Carnegie Hall and the Hollywood Bowl; exhibiting her surrealist pictures in art galleries for the benefit of the Red Cross; making pictures; doing a radio show; doing publicity work for

174

S. S. Van Dine's *The Gracie Allen Murder Case;*
writing a daily column in ninety newspapers . . .
you know, just something to keep her hand in.

So we were in conference, desperately trying to
think of something to keep this girl from getting
lazy, when one of my writers said, "She's done
everything but run for President of the United
States."

I gave him a raise and said, "That's it."

And Gracie was stuck again. This time, like the
Gracie's-brother routine, the publicity stunt snow-
balled far beyond anything we had planned on. We
started it, and the Union Pacific finished it. They
were about to celebrate their "Golden Spike Days"
in Omaha, an affair begun to commemorate the
opening of the first transcontinental railroad. Mr.
Jeffers, president of the Union Pacific, decided to
combine their publicity stunt with ours and he gave
us the bandwagon for Gracie's campaign. He presented us with a genuine Presidential train, complete with campaign platform, private rooms, dining
rooms, bathrooms with tubs—the works. The front
of the train was decorated with Gracie's emblem,
the kangaroo. The kangaroo was chosen as a mascot
of her "Surprise Party" because her campaign
motto was: "It's in the bag." She had a campaign
song, "Vote for Gracie," and we took along an orchestra to play it at all the stops.

The train started from Los Angeles, and made
whistle stops all the way across the country to
Omaha. Gracie's sister, Hazel Boyston, went along
with the rest of our entourage. (Entourage is a

word like nuance—just one on a page gives it a certain class.) We took hairdressers, wardrobe people, public-relations representatives, and writers. The writers and I worked day and night to dream up material for Gracie's speeches before we arrived at the next stop.

She was always met by the press, who demanded statements on world affairs. Samples: Her first statement was to call on all other candidates to withdraw. Her second was an appeal to the women— "Half the married couples in the United States are women," she said, "I repeat, half."

On the national debt: "It's something to be proud of; it's the biggest in the world, isn't it?"

Foreign relations: "They're all right with me, but when they come, they've just got to bring their own bedding."

On the Neutrality Bill: "If we owe it, let's pay it."

When asked if, when she became President, I would write for the papers, she said, "Don't be silly, if I'm President, he won't have to, we'll just send out for them."

We thought some of this was pretty funny, but Walter Winchell said it wasn't nearly as funny as the Republican and Democratic promises and speeches.

All the way across the country we were staggered by the crowds that met us at each stop. Thousands of people were at every station to meet us. We had a fantastic press. Even I got some good notices. One paper referred to me as "Glum-looking George

176

Burns," and another said, "Among those on the Campaign Special was George Burns, the candidate's stooge husband." I didn't sit up all night writing speeches for nothing.

We made thirty stops on the way to Omaha, and by the time we reached there, the people had really taken the campaign to heart. Menominee, Michigan, got confused and elected Gracie mayor, and Harvard University officially endorsed her. She was elected honorary princess of the Omaha Indian Tribe, became Wau-la-shja-wa, or "She who says funny things," and was given a war bonnet. I was given a feather and named Chief Pinfeather.

In Omaha, thirty thousand people came out to meet us in the pouring rain, and a parade formed to take us to the hotel. The front of the hotel had been changed to look like the White House. For three days Omaha turned itself upside down. We had dinners, lunches, a regular political convention in the Ak-Sar-Bar Coliseum, two national broadcasts, street dances, and an inaugural ball. We were guarded at all times by two detectives in eight-hour shifts. But Milton Berle stole some of our jokes anyway. Gracie got so used to these detectives being around that, late one night, she came out of her room to get a glass of milk and didn't see them, so she stuck her head out in the hall. There they were, very happy, being taught an Irish jig by Gracie's sister Hazel.

The celebration lasted four days. It was a terrible strain but terrific fun. We arrived back home exhausted. All Gracie wanted to do was lie down for a week and not open her mouth. But she had a surprise waiting for her. It was an invitation to attend First Lady's Night at the Washington Press Club in Washington, D. C.

Naturally, being exhausted, and knowing that because of work I couldn't go with her, she didn't want to go. Naturally, being Gracie, and the kind of a sport I referred to earlier, she went. My heart really ached for her—I knew what she was up against. Every newspaper in the country would be represented, and she was going not only without me, but, because of the short notice, without material, which was worse.

As I said, for a shy person Gracie landed in a great spot. In Washington she was in for another merry-go-round. She was photographed all over Washington in a variety of spots and with a variety of people, including Senate majority leader Alben Barkley.

The night of the dinner she was seated on the dais between Mrs. Harold Ickes and Mrs. Arthur Vandenberg. Gracie always dresses exquisitely, and this night was no exception. She wore what I think is called "a creation." Business having been good for some time, she had some magnificent jewelry— really quite a lot of diamonds by any standards, and she had them all on: after all, she was running for President.

She looked around, womanwise, to see what the other girls were wearing, and noticed a few gold wedding rings and a couple of wrist watches, and lots of plain black dresses. She was so embarrassed that she spent the rest of the dinner with one hand under the napkin to hide her bracelet and the other clasped over her shoulder to cover her brooch. She put her earrings and ring in her handbag. Feeling conspicuously out of place, being unprepared with proper material, being shy anyway as well as desperately tired, and being surrounded by a group of people famous in a different line of work from hers, Gracie didn't feel good. She was just beginning to wish she had stuck with Irish dancing, when someone patted her on the shoulder and said, "How's the future President?" It was Eleanor Roosevelt. Somehow she felt better.

Do you know, on election day, Gracie actually got a couple of hundred write-in votes on the ballot?

20

I F I seem to be jumping around chronologically, it's because I am. You haven't got the time to read about twenty years in Hollywood, and I haven't got time to write about it. The usual things happened, the kids' marks in school went up and down, our rating on radio went up and down, the kids got measles and mumps and got over them, Gracie got headaches and got over them, and I got a hacking cough—now that, I'll tell you about. If others want to talk about their operations, let them write their own biographies.

This cough was awful. You can imagine what a chronic hacking cough would do to someone in radio. And not only that, Gracie couldn't sleep nights because my hacking kept her up. Some nights I was good for twenty or thirty hacks an hour. I went to every doctor in town, looking for one who didn't say, "Stop smoking." All doctors, it seems, use the same writers. I remember one in particular. He had delivered the usual line about giving up smoking, when he was called from the room. I saw two boxes of cigars on his desk. While he was gone I emptied the boxes into my pockets. I don't know if you've ever put one hundred cigars into your pockets. It's not easy.

When the doctor came back I said, "Doctor, I think you're right, and I am going to quit. Now. This minute. Just to show you I mean what I say, I'm taking today's supply of cigars and leaving them right here." I took the hundred cigars from my pockets, put them on his desk, and walked out without waiting for his reaction. I stood outside the door and when I got my laugh I left.

I went from one doctor to another, trying to cure my cough. After I had tried all the Beverly Hills doctors, I heard about a man in downtown Los Angeles who was supposed to be great. I made an appointment and went to see him. When I walked into the waiting room there were about twenty people sitting there. I walked over to the nurse and said, "Will you please tell Dr. Ludwig that George Burns is outside?"

She disappeared through a door and came back in a couple of minutes and said, "He says to tell you that Dr. Ludwig is inside."

I sat down and waited my turn. When I was finally ushered into his office I was a hacking wreck.

Dr. Ludwig examined my throat and said, "What's your trouble?" I said, "I keep going around all the time hacking." He said, "Why do you do that?" That kind of a question I wasn't prepared for. "I don't know," I said. Ludwig said, "Stop it."

I said, "Stop it?" He said, "Yes, stop it. Don't do it anymore." I said, "That's all?" He said, "That's all." I said, "But aren't you going to give me something?" He said, "Do you want something?" I said, "Well, sure." He reached in his pocket. "Here's a piece of rock candy," he said. "Take this." As I walked out the door he said, "Mr. Burns." I said, "Yes?" He said, "Don't do that anymore."

Do you want to know something?—I never have.

Anyway, the children got older, and Sandy began to be surrounded by giants. All of them, every one of the boy friends, were absolute giants. There was one in particular—his name was Red; I used to run, but not fast enough, when I saw him. He always shook hands with me, and always nearly broke my hand. I finally took to keeping my hand in my pocket when he was calling, but that didn't stop him: he reached right in my pocket, grabbed my hand, and I was a southpaw again.

While Sandy was busy with her giants, Ronnie was going steady with a surfboard. He always has been beach-happy. As his grades in school went down, the sand content of our rugs went up. If they ever decide that sand is valuable and start to can it, we've got a corner on the market. Being worried about Ronnie's spending too much time at the beach, I decided to speak to him about it one day. I went at it kind of backhanded, as I always do when I'm trying to get something serious across. I didn't want him helping me with the lecture, and I figured if I could keep him confused until I got to the point, it would keep him off my side.

182

"Ronnie," I said, "I think we've been making a mistake. Education is no good. Trying to learn something, so that when you go out to earn a living you are prepared for life, is a lot of nonsense. I don't think you should waste any more time in school. At the present you're devoting your time to something far more important, and if you continue this way your grandchildren will have something to be proud of. Just think—I can see it now. . . . When you're seventy-five years old they'll be saying, 'That's my grandfather—he's the oldest surfboard rider in the world!' "

Ronnie didn't say much, but you could see it had affected him. The next day, he never even took his surfboard out of the garage. He went skin-diving instead.

Anyway, we were and are living in Beverly Hills. During the course of our lives here, we have engaged in the usual social activities, and generally had quite a good time. I had a great time when I was allowed to sing, but nobody else did.

I think there should be something mentioned here about Hollywood parties. They are nothing like what they're cracked up to be. People do not get drunk and fall into swimming pools, nobody drinks any champagne out of anybody else's slippers, and most handsome leading men have been paid to make love all day so they knock off at night. Parties are very big or very small. At the small ones, people either play cards, talk business, look at movies, or play scrabble—this last game is strictly for people who can spell. I play cards.

I Love Her, That's Why!

At the big parties, the guests are herded into a tent in the back yard which is decorated by a series of experts on flowers, lighting, dance floors, balloons, etc. There are enough big parties so that this group of experts can make a good living doing nothing but putting parties together. The costume party is the least popular type. Actors don't like to dress up—they've had it. At the big parties dancing keeps men and women together. At the small ones all the women drift to one side of the room, and all the men to another—don't ask me why, they just do.

At both kinds of parties nobody is ever on time, which is what makes it hard on Gracie and me. Being vaudevillians, we instinctively get there first, to get rehearsal check Number One, and no matter how hard we've tried in our years out here, if we're asked for eight o'clock, we get there at eight, and spend the next forty-five minutes driving around the block until somebody else arrives.

Once we're in, I have no trouble socially. If the line, "A funny thing happened on the way to the party," doesn't stir up some response in one guest, I drop him and project at another one. I can generally find a fresh audience for a few jokes, and if one of those intellectuals tries to draw me into a discussion, I have a perfect answer for him. I go home.

Gracie has a harder time—she's nicer than I am, and she always talks to the wrong people. If Clark Gable and Robert Taylor are sitting on a couch on one side of the room, and somebody's aunt from Iowa is on the other, she's going to go and talk to the aunt, because she feels sorry for her. She knows

184

Clark Gable and Robert Taylor aren't going to have any trouble finding someone to talk to, and the aunt is. The upshot of it is, Gracie always goes home from a party with a headache because she's worked so hard trying to give someone else a good time.

Like anything else, the first Hollywood party is the hardest; at least it certainly was in our case. We had come out to do our first "Big Broadcast" picture for Paramount, and Manny Cohen, head of production at Paramount, invited us to a party for Rocky and Gary Cooper. We were asked for seven-thirty, and as the house was up in the hills, and as I was just learning to drive, we started at seven. It was quite a drive. I'm no good now, and this was twenty-three years ago. It was a nerve-racking trip. Nobody who can't yodel should live so high up.

When we arrived at the house it was dark, there was no sign of life, except a large police dog who charged out barking and wouldn't let us out of the car. I backed the car out with some difficulty, and we drove around in the hills to kill some more time. Half an hour later we took another stab at it. There were no other cars yet, but this time the lights were on, and the police dog wasn't, so I said to Gracie, "Shall we try it?" She said, "Why not? It won't be the first time we ever played to an empty house." It was now eight o'clock.

As I stopped the car the police dog ran out of the house, barking. We jumped back in the car, and then we saw that the dog was followed by a butler. The butler held onto the dog's collar. He looked surprised, but he was very polite. After ushering us in, he took our wraps and disappeared upstairs. He came back, followed by our host who was in a bathrobe.

By the look Manny Cohen gave us, I was certain that he would have torn up our contracts if he'd had them handy. But being a charming man, he said to have a drink and he'd be down in a minute. Gracie looked at me, I looked at her; we were both so embarrassed we couldn't speak. The butler brought us a couple of martinis. Now Gracie doesn't drink at all, and I'm not a martini man, myself, but we drank those two drinks as if they were the last two there were going to be. The butler brought us two more. They went down the same way. Then he brought us two more. Gracie didn't drink the third. She said, "This is awful. I don't feel well." I said, "Go into the dressing room." She went into the dressing room and went to sleep. I drank her martini.

Now I was all alone. I took a walk in the garden and met that police dog again. This time he was very pleasant. He must have figured if I had gotten by the butler I was all right. I was so glad to have someone to talk to that I sat down and talked to that dog for about twenty minutes. I told him some of my best shaggy-dog stories but never got a snicker. In fact, he killed the point of one of them by running off to bark at the doorbell.

The first arrival after us was Barbara Stanwyck, and I asked her if she would go in and get Gracie. While I waited for the girls to come out, the butler handed me another martini. By the end of the fifth, I had not only gotten over being embarrassed, but I was doing imitations. By the sixth, I was convinced I was a riot. By the seventh, I was convinced I was the host, but the host convinced me I wasn't and suggested I go home. I'm not saying that the martinis affected me, but at one point, I picked up a cigar, took out my lighter, lit the lighter, threw away the cigar, threw away the lighter, and put a match in my mouth.

The next morning Gracie felt fine, because she had stopped at the second martini and had that refreshing little nap in the dressing room. I can't describe how I felt. I didn't want Gracie to know how bad it was, so I said, "You stay in bed—I'll make breakfast." I worked with speed and efficiency, put the water on to boil for coffee, made orange juice, took the eggs out of the refrigerator, put the bread in the toaster, got it a perfect golden brown, and put it under the faucet and washed it. Those martinis won't let go.

After we had lived here for a while, we gave a party ourselves, for Blossom Seeley, Benny Fields, and Damon Runyon. Every comedian was there; I don't think we missed one. Gracie was worried about the caterers and the decoration. I wasn't worried about anything. I had hired a good piano player, and at a party with this kind of a cast, if you've got a piano player with a good bass hand, you've got a party. Something I forgot to tell you is that in Hollywood everybody entertains. If you've got a stunt, you are bound to be asked, and happy to do it. The day of this party, I ran into Phil Silvers who had just come into town. Silvers, in case you don't know it, is only one of the funniest men in the world, and he can't walk in the door of a party without being asked to do something.

I said, "Phil, I want you to come to a party tonight and I promise you, you won't be asked to entertain." Phil said, "This, I don't believe." I said, "Phil, I promise you." "Okay," he said. "Thanks, I'll come."

That night I was a perfect host. I waited a full hour before I sang even one note. Then everybody got on: Groucho Marx sang Gilbert and Sullivan, Harpo Marx played the piano, Jack Benny played the violin, Blossom Seeley sang "Toddling the Toodle," Benny Fields sang "Melancholy Baby," George Jessel sang "Mother's Eyes," Meredith Willson played some of his own numbers, Eddie Cantor sang "If You Knew Susie," and then Lou Holtz was singing "The Monkey Rag" and was singing his heart out when the butler started to empty the ash trays. Holtz was so mad that he kicked the butler in the seat of the pants. He never stopped singing, and the butler never stopped emptying the ash trays. At the finish of the number, we all applauded, and Holtz went to the kitchen and brought the butler back for a bow.

I was in the middle of "In the Heart of a Cherry," my fourth number—yes, I said fourth—after all, I paid for the piano player, when Phil Silvers came up to me and said, "George, I can't stand it any longer, I've just got to get on!"

By two o'clock Phil was still on, and I was tired, so I said, "How would you all like to go to Ciro's?" The guests said they'd love it. They started to get their coats, and when they were all outside I said, "All right, you go to Ciro's—I'm going to bed." And I closed the door. Phil Silvers did two more numbers in the street, and they left.

Simon and Schuster just called me from New York. They said, "We like the last few chapters you sent, but try to remember, this isn't *Gone with the Wind.*" Those publishers are real subtle; they mean it's getting too long. I think they're making a big mistake. Anything over 80,000 words they don't have to pay me for anyway, so you'd think they'd be glad to get a few extra ones. They're going to need them. They're going to publish Jack Benny's book, and he's so stingy that if they tell him 80,000 words, that's just what they'll get: 80,000 words, not one comma more. Anyway, they hollered stop, so I'll only tell you about two more parties—the maddest, and the shortest.

The maddest was given for us by John P. Medbury. The entrance to his house was through a tent-covered walk. At the end of the walk was a man in a bathtub taking a bath. He said, "The party is that way." All around the house there were pickets walking, carrying signs saying "Don't go to this party." There were men sitting in the trees in the yard, dressed in white tie and tails, and they were fishing. As you passed the garage you could see inside. It was fixed up like a bedroom and there was a beautiful girl dressed in a black negligee standing outside winking at the men as they passed. During the course of the evening, every half hour a page boy walked through the house announcing, "It is now eight-thirty." At ten o'clock a man dressed in knee britches made a half-hour speech in Polish. There were two-way mikes installed in the powder rooms so if you went in one with someone and said, "When do you suppose we are going to eat?" a voice came back saying, "When it's ready." Olson and Johnson arrived on stretchers, in an ambulance. Also this party took place in July and there was a Christmas tree and an angry Santa Claus sitting by it who, if you touched anything on the tree, hit you with a stick. Everybody played the part perfectly. I think Medbury must have had a rehearsal. At four o'clock when Gracie and I went home the page was still announcing, "It is now eight-thirty."

The shortest party I referred to—and I may say the saddest—was one we gave for the Jack Bennys. I told them to wear dinner clothes. When they arrived there was just us and six musicians. They kept looking around for new arrivals, but nobody came. Because nobody was invited. Just us, the Bennys, and six musicians. During cocktails the Bennys kept looking expectantly toward the door. When we sat down to dinner, Jack couldn't stand it any longer. He said, "Is this the party?"

I said, "This is it."

"Just us and six musicians?" he said.

"That's it," I said.

Not a snicker out of Jack, and I had thought it would kill him. It's bad enough to lay an egg, but to lay an egg when you've paid for six musicians—it's painful. We suffered through dinner and went into the living room for coffee—followed by the musi-

190

cians. We drank our coffee almost in silence, and suddenly Jack, who couldn't stand it any longer, said, "How would you like to go to the movies?" The musicians said, "We'd love to." So the ten of us went to a show.

This may sound like a lie, but it's only because the first half of it isn't true and the last half I had to make up to keep it believable.

21

I HATE to admit it, but every important thing in our lives that I wanted to do and Gracie didn't, I tricked her into doing. Like marrying me. It worked the first time, and I'm afraid I've done it a lot since.

I remember one time in particular. We were offered a picture which starred Fred Astaire. The parts we were to play called for us to do a dance with him. Now, if you remember, I started doing a talking act because the chorus girls could outdance me, so I knew my dancing with Astaire would be like Jack Benny playing a duet with Jascha Heifetz. I also knew that Gracie was good enough to dance with him, if she would. I also knew she probably wouldn't, because she never has realized how good she is, and she didn't want to work in pictures anyway.

I had a three-way problem: I had to trick Gracie into trying out for the part, I had to trick Astaire into thinking we were better than we were, and I

192

had to trick myself into thinking I could outthink both of them. I had ten days to get this trick going before we were to dance for Astaire. First, I got Gracie's O.K. This time it wasn't hard, because I convinced her there was no possibility of our getting the Astaire picture. I just said, "Gracie, isn't this ridiculous? Us dancing with Astaire? You could do it, of course, but with me we don't stand a chance. We'll never get the job, but it might be fun trying." She went along with this.

My next move was to try and locate two fellers who used to do a whisk-broom dance in vaudeville. They were just great. One of them had retired, but I located the other, paid him for the rights to the dance and for his time while he taught it to us. Gracie is a great Irish dancer, and this thing was a natural for her. As usual, she had no idea how good she was.

When the time was up, we had our appointment with Astaire. The three of us walked in: Gracie, me, and the whisk-broom expert. We did the dance for Fred and he said, "It's great! It goes in the picture just the way it is." The psychology was perfect. I had located a dance Fred hadn't seen (some trick to begin with), and neither Gracie nor I were nervous about dancing with him, because instead of his teaching us, we were teaching him.

More or less the same technique worked to get Gracie into television. When television first came in, our agency, M.C.A., thought we should go into it, and fast—get in on the ground floor, I think is what they said. I agreed with them. Gracie didn't.

193

I Love Her, That's Why!

"This is one thing," she said, shaking her head, "that I will not be pushed into."

So I just pushed her a little. I said, "Googie, do me one favor. Before you shake your head the other way, listen to me. TV is here—there's no use pretending that it isn't. Let us make one TV test—no tricks; I'll shoot all your angles, good and bad, so you'll see the worst that can happen."

She said, "I'll buy that, but if I don't like the test, it's out." I already knew we were in. Along with never realizing how talented she is, Gracie doesn't really know how pretty she is. I figured if we could show her, the battle was won.

The next move was to decide on a format for the show. I had lunch at Romanoff's with Bill Paley, president of C.B.S., Harry Ackerman, vice-president of C.B.S., and Taft Schreiber, vice-president of M.C.A., Micky Rockford, vice-president of M.C.A., and Mike Levee, vice-president of M.C.A. Incidentally, those initials, M.C.A. and C.B.S., stand for Music Corporation of America and Columbia Broadcasting System. Vice-president stands for v.p. I was pretty embarrassed; I was the only one at the table with no title. Anyway, we had this lunch conference about what kind of a show it was going to be. All the boys had ideas. I sat there doing straight for them. It's hard for me to be anything else. For years, in our act, Gracie would say something, I'd repeat it, she'd answer it, and get her laugh. From force of habit I repeat everything. In fact, I've been a straight man for so many years that when I went fishing with a feller one day, and he fell overboard and yelled, "Help!" I said, "Help?"—and while I waited for him to get his laugh, he drowned. This is a joke I used once in my monologue, and it got a big laugh. And as I'm not writing this book to make you cry, I thought I'd try it again.

Anyway, we were at Romanoff's, and it was Paley who gave us the hook that we decided to hang the show on. He said, "George, I understand you make a lot of speeches at stag dinners. Why couldn't you do a little monologue on the show?" I said, "I could. And what do you think of the idea of a domestic comedy, with us living in Beverly Hills, where we do, with a dividing line between the actors and the audience, so I can talk to the audience—sort of step over the line and let them in on it?" Everybody applauded me for five minutes, and that was that.

If we are successful, it is because we don't play down to an audience—we don't believe in that. There has been foolish talk about audiences having an average twelve-year-old mind: it just isn't true. They are older than anybody, and wiser. And what is more, every individual among them is a manager, because in this day of television he owns his own theater. The first thing an actor learns is to get along with the manager. He does well when he doesn't forget it.

Anyway, I got together with my writers and we established the format we use today for our pilot film. Ralph Levy, one of the smartest young men in television, directed it, and he did a wonderful job. Gracie looked so pretty, she couldn't help but O.K. it, and we were in business. We showed the film to

195

the Carnation Company. They bought it, and we've been with them ever since. We are now cosponsored by the B. F. Goodrich Rubber Company. We did a live show every other week for two years.

The third year, we decided to put the show on film and do it weekly. I like this arrangement better, because every week is habit-forming; you don't have a chance to cool off between shows; and what is more important, it makes it possible to take your show out of town before opening on Broadway. By this I mean that we preview our shows before a live audience, before we put them on television. That laughter you hear is the real thing; we record it at the preview.

If, at these previews, we're unlucky and a joke lays an egg, we cut in a chuckle—about what the joke is worth. In other words, we allow it to lay an egg, but not a complete egg. Fortunately, our writers being good ones, this situation doesn't come up often. Sometimes, in fact, it works in reverse, and the laughter is so big we have to cut the tail off it because the audience can't hear the next straight line. If there is one thing I do have a talent for, it is knowing where laughs will come, so our timing when shooting the picture is geared to wait for them.

We use a two-camera technique in filming the show. If you like, I can explain it to you. (Come to think of it, you don't have much choice.) It works this way: Say Gracie is telling me a joke. I react to that joke; she takes a vase of flowers and walks out of the frame, or the range, of the first camera. The first camera stays on my reaction; the second follows her to a table where she places the vase. When we show the film, it is only from the first camera, which is my reaction to Gracie's joke. If we have bad luck and the joke doesn't get a laugh, we use the film from the second camera—Gracie with the vase of flowers—to fill in where the laugh should be, so we don't have to use a phony unless it's absolutely necessary. In other words, the empty spot is covered by a piece of perfectly legitimate business, so you don't miss it. If there isn't any laugh, that's perfectly O.K.—there's not supposed to be anything funny about putting a vase of flowers on a table.

The approach Gracie and I use in working in front of a camera is entirely different. I always play to an audience, just as I did when we were on the stage. Gracie doesn't, and never did. To her, the footlights are the fourth wall of a room—the audience; and in this case the cameras do not exist. She reads her lines completely instinctively, as if she were in her own living room, and never looks across the footlights.

I'll never forget the time she varied a fraction from this. We were doing a live show—she was in the middle of a scene—and something made her accidentally peek at the camera. She suddenly stopped dead in her tracks, then went on with her dialogue. After the show she pointed to the camera and said, "What's that little red light on the camera?" The director looked at her like she had two heads. He said, "Gracie, we have three cameras—that means that one is on. All live cameras have a red light on—you've been playing in front of one for a year and a half." She said, "Turn it off—I never want to see it again, it scares me."

Gracie also has a special approach to a script. As I said, her readings are instinctive, and we never put any stage directions in her scripts, such as [*Pause*]. She might pause for three days. This instinct for readings is what makes her the success she is, and it is the fact that she is unconscious of them that keeps them charming.

Once we were playing B. F. Keith's Theater in Newark, and Jack Benny was on the bill with us. One night he said, "Gracie, you kill me with the way you read that line: 'Yes, but my father wouldn't let you kiss my mother.' I love it so much that I'm in the wings every night just to hear it." That joke was out from then on. She tried to do it the way Jack liked it, and couldn't ever do it again. So we just turn her loose and let her do it her way. In my opinion, it's about as good a way as you can get. Now if Benny will stay out of the wings, and if people will stop complimenting Gracie, we'll get something accomplished.

We try to keep getting something fresh into the show. It's hard to stay up there, when people are as used to you as they are to us. Youngsters in the business can be molded into something different, and can try new tricks. We're pretty much stuck with what we are, so we can't ever let down in our efforts to make what we are as entertaining as possible.

I hate to tell the truth, because it never gets a laugh, but we do accomplish something in shooting

198

the show in one day. The major studios feel they've done a great day's work if they shoot four or five pages of dialogue in a day. We shoot forty-three. Now don't get me wrong. The majors aren't having any trouble; this is just a comparison.

When we shoot, I want Gracie to know her lines perfectly, which she always does, but I don't want the other actors to. I want the audience to feel the actors cooking; if there is a hesitation, or even if they muff a line, it makes it seem more like a live show.

The method by which we can get the show on film in one day is by rehearsing in continuity on Tuesday, line for line just as it is in the script, so everybody knows exits and entrances and attitudes; then Wednesday we shoot, not in continuity, but according to the way our sets are lined up, which is like an assembly line. The sets are always lit, so all we have to do is move in a few key lights, turn on the switch, and the actors are cooking.

All of us have been together like a family for a long time, and it has been a pleasure to work with such a pleasant and competent group of people, and that's as much as I'll say about them, for fear they'll see this and want a raise. There's Freddy de Cordova, our producer-director; Phil Tannura, our cameraman; Harry Von Zell, who announces and plays himself; Bea Benadaret, who plays Blanche Morton, and has been with us since radio; and Larry Keating, who plays Harry Morton. These people are all tops, and we're lucky to have them. Larry is the youngest member of the family. Fred Clark, also a fine actor, who used to play Morton, left us to go with a Broadway show. We had no trouble getting the public to accept another Harry Morton, because we leveled with them, as usual.

Larry's first day in the show had a scene in which Blanche was supposed to be waiting by the door to hit Harry over the head with a telephone book when he came in. I walked into the scene and said, "Hold it!" Then I explained about Fred leaving the show, and introduced Larry to them. Then I introduced Larry to Bea Benadaret. They bowed, and I said, "Now, let's get back to the story." Bea went back to her book, Larry made his entrance, Bea hit him over the head, and we had a new Harry Morton.

Jerry Boggio, our secretary, has been with us fifteen years. Some mornings I come in, and if I had looked at our show on TV the night before and didn't think it came off, I come in and I'm mad at myself and at everybody else. I may yell at my brother Willie, or it may be at Jerry. I never say what's on my mind, just yell—something like, "Why aren't those windows washed?" Jerry just says, "I'll have the windows washed right away, but I *liked* last night's show." This kind of understanding is invaluable in someone who runs interference for you. Jerry knows without asking, who we can see, how many benefits we can do, what time to allot to appointments (and keeps me from forgetting them); she calls the cook and reminds her to put the meat in, and is official go-between with the children. If we want them to do something and want it handled subtly, we have Jerry do it. She doesn't know we know she does the same for them. An all-around doll, this girl—and pretty, too. She started at twenty-two dollars a week, and last month she fired me twice.

Our writers are my brother Willie Burns, Harvey Helm, Sid Dorfman, and Keith Fowler. Incidentally, my brother Willie hasn't got an easy life. If the rating is down, it's Willie's fault. If it's up, I'm wearing a red tie. If the writers can't think of an idea, it's Willie's fault. When Willie thinks of an idea, I'm wearing a red tie. Around option time, if it looks as if the sponsor is not going to renew, it's Willie's fault. When the sponsor does renew, I'm wearing a red, white and blue tie.

This would be a good time to say something about writers. This group of ours generally look more as if they were going to a funeral instead of a story conference. And there's a reason. Writers of a comedy show don't sit around and make jokes and laugh. The only thing we laugh at, generally, when we're working, is something that doesn't go into the script. Writing is a murderous job. You have a deadline to begin with, and when you're trying to knock out a situation and it just doesn't jell, there's no quitting, because some genius isn't going to drop in and fix it for you. You have just so much time in which to get it on paper, and you stay there until you fix it yourself.

Frequently we come to a dead end. Nobody can think of anything, and we sit and stare at each other knowing we aren't going to get out of that room until somebody comes up with an idea. We sit and sweat and stare, and then suddenly somebody says, "What if—?" and then we stare some more. Then somebody says, "What if—?" again. More staring, more "what if?s" and then suddenly you've got it, sometimes after hours of staring and iffing. Somebody says something we all spark to. Everybody talks at once, and so fast you can't even get it down on paper.

It was this kind of "what if?" that led to the script I'm about to show you. I thought you might like to see how it looks on paper instead of a television screen. Jerry came in when we were in conference and said the publishers (I'm not going to mention those two fellers' names again) wanted some baby pictures for this book. I said, "As soon as I can get time to open my trunks, I'll look for some." One of my writers said, "That's an idea for a show. There should be a lot of funny things in that trunk." And here it is:

Film Show #125   Filmed: January 12, 1955
(Carnation)   Shown: February 21, 1955

The George Burns and Gracie Allen Show

FIRST REVISION

CAST:
George Burns
Gracie Allen
Harry Von Zell
Bea Benadaret
(Blanche Morton)
Larry Keating
(Harry Morton)
Mr. Cannon
Ned Brown
Dr. Bellamy

SETS:
Front of Burns House
Den
Burns Bedroom
Burns Living Room
Burns Patio
Morton Front Door
Morton Living Room

WRITTEN BY:
Sid Dorfman
Harvey Helm
Keith Fowler
William Burns

PRODUCED AND DIRECTED BY:
Frederick de Cordova
ASSOCIATE PRODUCER:
Al Simon

203

[*Dissolve to: Front of Burns house. Gracie* in house dress is supervising as Mr. Cannon *puts in rosebushes. He's digging a hole at the side of the porch.*]

Cannon:

I think you'll be pleased with these rosebushes.

Gracie:

I'm sure I will be. How much do I owe you? I'll get the money from my husband.

Cannon:

No hurry. The bushes aren't in yet, and this ground is pretty hard.

Gracie:

Even so . . . I'm sure you can get them into the hard ground quicker than I can get the money from George.

Cannon:

[*Laughs*] Okay . . . the whole thing comes to nine dollars, including the tax.

[Blanche *comes in wearing an apron.*]

Blanche:

Hi, Gracie.

Gracie:

Oh, good morning, Blanche.

I Love Her, That's Why!

[Cannon *continues working.*]

Blanche:

I just came over. . . . Oh, your rosebushes have come.

Gracie:

Yes.

Blanche:

Wait till you hear this! I just got a phone call **from** Lucille Vanderlip, and she told me Margie Bates got a beautiful diamond bracelet from her husband.

Gracie:

I can't believe it.

Blanche:

Why not?

Gracie:

If Lucille's husband gave another woman a diamond bracelet, you'd think she'd be the last one to mention it.

[Cannon *looks around . . . looks at* Blanche.]

Blanche:

Er . . . Gracie . . . you misunderstood me.

[*Cut to: As* Harry *opens Mortons' door.*]

Harry:

Blanche! I've got to get to work. What about my eggs?

Blanche:
[*Off*] They're on and cooking.

Harry:
Blanche . . . when will you learn . . . by three-minute eggs I mean. . . .
[Blanche *walks in.*]

Blanche:
[*Mocking*] I know . . . you mean they should be cooked three minutes—not cooked so it takes three minutes to break into them.

Harry:
That is precisely what I mean.
[Gracie *walks up to them.*]

Gracie:
[*Gaily*] Good morning, Harry.

Harry:
Good morning, Gracie.

Blanche:
[*Sotto*] I'll be back as soon as I feed old Sourpuss here.

Gracie:
All right. [*To Harry*] Have a nice breakfast, Sourpuss.
[Harry *glares.* Blanche *reacts.*]

Blanche:
Er . . . er . . . I'll see you later.

207

[Blanche *scoots around* Harry *and inside.* Harry *follows.* Gracie *turns and calls toward the back of the house.*]

Gracie:

George. . . .

George:

[*Off*] Yeah?

Gracie:

Would you come down and pay the gardener?

[*Cut to: Den.* George *is calling out side door of den.*]

George:

I'll be down in a few minutes.

[George *turns back into the room.* Ned Brown *is there.*]

Well, look, Ned, I know I've got some baby pictures some place around here, but I don't know where to put my hands on them.

Ned:

George, the publishers have got to have them. Since the first couple of chapters of your book are about your childhood, these pictures are going to be used to illustrate it. And I've got to air-mail them to New York within the next twenty-four hours.

George:

Well, I'll find them and phone you.

Ned:

All right.

[Ned *starts out. Stops when he sees picture of* George *with seal.*]

Hey, here's an interesting picture. We ought to use this.

George:

Oh, that's a vaudeville act I used to do. It was called "Flipper and Burns."

[*Camera shows picture.*]

Ned:

Working with a seal? How did a big talent wind up with a partner like that?

George:

I'll admit Flipper was clever, but don't forget, on closing nights I did all the packing.

Ned:

[*Laughs*] How did you decide to do an act like that? How do you go about getting a seal?

George:

Well, I was living in this little theatrical hotel, and the fellow next door to me had an animal act. He had trained ducks, pigeons, rabbits, and a seal. Things were tough and he started eating his act.

Ned:

He did?

I Love Her, That's Why!

George:
Yeah, he ate the ducks, the pigeons, and started on the rabbits. I came home one night and found the seal hiding under my bed.

Ned:
George, is that true?

George:
No, it's a lie, but I'm putting it in the book.

Ned:
[*Laughs*] So long, George, and don't forget those baby pictures. They're important.

George:
I'll start looking for them right away.

[Ned *goes.*]

[*Dissolve to: Front of Burns House.* Gracie *and* Cannon.]

Gracie:
Not that I'm worried, Mr. Cannon, but have you had any experience planting things in this neighborhood?

Cannon:
Oh, sure, I put in some things for Mrs. Bagley across the street.

Gracie:
Well, this is a peculiar street. The climate is different over there.

210

[Cannon *pauses in his work.*]

Cannon:
It is?

Gracie:
Oh, yes. You see, in the afternoon we get the sun in the front yard . . . and over there they get it in the back yard.

Cannon:
Oh, I see.

Gracie:
And in the morning it's just the opposite.

Cannon:
Well, don't worry, Mrs. Burns. This is the best place for the roses.

[George *comes in.*]

George:
Oh, hello.

Cannon:
Hello.

George:
How much do we owe you?

Cannon:
Nine dollars, including tax.

[George *takes out his money.*]

I Love Her, That's Why!

George:

Here's ten.

[George *notes his money.*]

That's funny.

Gracie:

What?

[Cannon *gives* George *a dollar.*]

George:

I cashed a twenty-five-dollar check last night. I spent five and I just gave him ten. I should have ten left, but I've only got five. I wonder what happened to that other five.

Gracie:

How do you like the new roses?

George:

Fine . . . I know I didn't spend it. . . . Maybe I dropped it up in the den.

[George *starts out.*]

Cannon:

Thank you, and good-by, Mr. Burns.

[George *doesn't answer.*]

Gracie:

George.

George:

What?

Gracie:

Aren't you going to say good-by?

[George *is gone.*]

George:

[*Off*] Good-by, sweetheart.

Gracie:

He called you sweetheart. That five dollars has really got him upset. I'd better go in and look around the house for it.

Cannon:

Yeah, little things like that can do it. A friend of mine mislaid a five-dollar bill once.. Didn't know whether he spent it or lost it or what. He couldn't get his mind off it. He stopped in the middle of the street to think about it. A truck driver honked his horn at him. Next thing he knew he was down an open manhole.

Gracie:

The truck driver must have had something on his mind, too, or he wouldn't have driven his truck down an open manhole.

[Gracie *goes.* Cannon *reacts.*]

Cannon:

Yeah . . . I guess he did.

[*Dissolve to: Monologue.*]

George:

I hope I find those baby pictures before the show is over. I'd like to show them to you. There's one of me you'll get a kick out of. I'm stretched out on a bear-skin rug smoking a cigar. . . . You don't believe it, huh? Well, you're right. It was actually a rabbitskin rug. We were very poor. . . . But the people down the street didn't have to use any rugs. They had a Shetland pony. They were very rich. No children . . . just four Shetland ponies. . . .

Nowadays when they take pictures of babies, they don't pose them any more. It's all candid shots. The baby has to be doing something. The trouble is that most of the things a two-month-old baby can do don't make for a good picture. . . . And these candid photographers must take about eight thousand pictures. . . . And by the time you pick out a picture that you like, the kid is old enough to take a picture of his own baby. . . .

I haven't found the pictures yet, but I sure found some useful stuff that I've saved through the years. Like a menu from the Swedish Restaurant at the St. Louis Exposition . . . thirty-three keys with no locks . . . and a mother-of-pearl banjo pick. And they'll come in very handy if I ever run into a Swede who can't unlock his banjo. . . .

I also found a penny that I've kept for sentimental reasons. It was the first penny I ever got when I started singing on street corners as a kid. I didn't save the penny because it was the first one I ever earned. I saved it because it was given to me by the Indian whose picture is on it. . . . The Indian didn't really give me the penny. He heard me sing and he hit me with it. . . .

Everybody collects useless things. I knew a fellow

who couldn't throw out a piece of wrapping paper. His basement was full of wrapping paper—saved it for years. His wife told him to stop, but he said sometime it might come in handy for Christmas presents . . . and it did. Last Christmas he gave each of his friends fifteen pounds of wrapping paper. . . .

But women are sentimental about the stuff they keep. A friend of mine has been married about twenty years, and he told me that his wife kept the first flower he ever gave her, pressed in a book. It fell out of the book last night when she hit him over the head with it. . . .

Gracie is sentimental, too. She saved the first piece of candy I ever gave her. I'd like to show it to you. But I can't open the book. . . .

Then there are some people we know back East who lived in a big house on Long Island. They lived there for thirty years, and finally they sold the place. And when they moved, they went down in the basement and they couldn't get over all the junk they accumulated. Not only that—they found out their son hadn't run away from home in 1940, after all. . . .

Take my Uncle Frank . . . he collected tons of junk and he couldn't bear to part with any of it. That's why he went broke. He was a junk man. . . . Well, I'd better get to looking for those pictures. Oh, I guess you're worrying about that fellow who's been down in the basement since 1940. Without any windows or doors, I guess you're wondering how he got any air. He had a hole in his pants. . . .

I Love Her, That's Why!

[*Dissolve to: Den.* George *is hunting through his papers, drawers, etc., for the baby pictures. Everything is in a mess.* Gracie *comes in.*]

Gracie:

George, have you found the five dollars?

George:

No, I don't know what happened to it. Gracie, I had a flock of baby pictures. Do you know where they are?

Gracie:

They're around somewhere. Why?

George:

I need them.

Gracie:

Then you ought to look for them instead of the five dollars.

George:

Yeah, that's a good idea.

[George *takes a grip from the closet, opens it. Papers in it.*]

Gracie:

Sure. You can't worry about little things. First thing you know you'll lose your mind, and that's certainly not worth five dollars. Worrying about little things can get you in real trouble. Look at that friend of Mr. Cannon's. How would you like it if

216

you stopped in the middle of the street to think about five dollars, and a truck driver honked at you, and the next thing you know he was down an open manhole.

George:

Who?

Gracie:

You. No one else is here, and I hope you don't think I'm talking to myself.

George:

What am I doing down an open manhole?

Gracie:

I don't know. I don't even know what the truck driver was doing down there.

George:

Truck driver?

Gracie:

He honked at Mr. Cannon's friend. You know, the one you called sweetheart.

[Gracie *goes* . . . *Returns.*]

George, I don't like to see you upset. So before I go, promise me you'll forget what we've been talking about.

George:

That should be easy. What have we been talking about?

217

I Love Her, That's Why!

Gracie:

That's good, dear. You've forgotten already.

> [Gracie *leaves, leaving the door open*
> . . . George *turns to camera.*]

George:

I don't know who the truck driver is, but if I called him sweetheart, maybe he's got my baby pictures.

> [*Dissolve to: Morton living room.*
> Blanche *and* Harry.]

Blanche:

I can't get over George being so upset about losing five dollars. Why should a man with all his money worry about that? For him it's just a drop in the bucket.

Harry:

That's the attitude of an extravagant person, Blanche. It's your habit to turn the bucket upside down and drain it.

Blanche:

Oh, now I'm extravagant!

Harry:

Now, in the past, and—I fear—in the future.

Blanche:

Well, I like that!

Harry:

I'm sure you do, but it sickens me.

Blanche:

[*Mimics*] "It sickens me! It sickens me!" Oh, I wish I was a man! I'd knock some of that pompousness out of you.

Harry:

Yes, it's too bad you're not a man. We might have been good friends.

Blanche:

Let me tell you. . . .

> [Harry *and* Blanche *look at each other and start to laugh.* Gracie *comes in.*]

Hi, honey. Has George found his five dollars?

Gracie:

No, and he's making such a fuss about it. When my Cousin Otis misplaced his automobile he didn't carry on that much. George's den looks like it was hit by a cyclone.

Harry:

Your Cousin Otis misplaced his automobile?

Gracie:

Yes. He'd always walk off and forget where he parked it. So he finally tied one end of a rope to the rear bumper and the other end around his waist, and it worked fine until he got a traffic ticket.

Blanche:

He got a traffic ticket?

I Love Her, That's Why!

Gracie:

Yes, while he was out of the car somebody stole it and dragged him right through a red light.

Blanche:

[*Chuckles*] You're right. Then George shouldn't worry.

Harry:

I was going over to tell George that I can't keep our golf date. And while I'm there, Gracie, I'll take the opportunity to give him a friendly lecture on financial carelessness. It may prove decidedly beneficial.

Gracie:

Not only that. It might do some good.

Harry:

Yes, it might.

[*He goes out.*]

[*Cut to: Den.* George *is still hunting.* Harry *comes in, looks around. Den is now more upset. More grips out.*]

Harry:

George, I came over to inform you I can't play golf this afternoon.

George:

Why tell me? You never could.

Harry:

That was scarcely an example of scintillating drollery.

220

George:

Well, what do you expect from a straight man?

> [George *continues to look.* Harry *reacts to it.*]

Harry:

Gracie tells me you misplaced five dollars.

George:

Yeah . . . I don't remember what happened to it.

Harry:

The trouble with you, George, is that you have an overwhelming tendency toward negligence and a dangerous disregard for the ordinary precepts of methodology.

George:

Well, if I've got that, no wonder I can't remember things. I'm a sick man.

Harry:

I mean that you're not systematic. I could never lose anything, because my daily routine is carefully arranged. For example, I know exactly how much I have in my wallet, because I make a mental note of all my expenditures.

George:

That's your business, Harry.

Harry:

Now, yesterday I was downtown auditing some books. When I left the house I had the sum of twenty-one dollars with me. My lunch cost me a dollar and twenty-five cents at the Sunshine Health Food Restaurant.

George:
Sounds like a great place to eat.

Harry:
It's always been my favorite. I had a mushroom sandwich on gluten bread, a chopped water-cress and brazil-nut salad and a glass of papaya juice . . . an excellent meal for the price. I then stopped in. . . .

George:
You did say papaya juice?

Harry:
Yes. Then I stopped in. . . .

George:
And gluten bread?

Harry:
Yes. Then I stopped in. . . .

George:
Do they take New Year's Eve reservations?

Harry:
I'll inquire.

George:
Thanks.

222

Harry:

I then stopped in at a bookstore and paid three seventy-five for a book I have long wished to read: "The Flora and Fauna of the Lower Mississippi Basin." George, if you ever care to borrow it. . . .

George:

Well, I'll take it with me New Year's Eve. It'll go nicely with that gluten bread.

Harry:

My last stop was at my barber's where I had a singe and an egg shampoo. The cost was three dollars—making a total outlay of eight dollars for the day.

George:

And what a day it must have been!

Harry:

Eight dollars from twenty-one dollars leaves thirteen dollars . . . which I now have in my wallet.

[*He takes out wallet and counts bills.*]

Five—ten—eleven—twelve—thirteen—fourteen. . . . Good heavens, where did that extra dollar come from?

George:

Anything can happen to a guy who drinks papaya juice.

Harry:

This is very disturbing. It has never happened to me before.

I Love Her, That's Why!

[George *takes dollar and puts it in his pocket.*]

George:

Now I'm only out four dollars and you've got nothing to be disturbed about.

[*He goes out. Camera stays on* Harry, *looking dazed.*]

[*Dissolve to: Commercial.*]

[*Dissolve to: George.*]

George:

Looking for my baby pictures, this trunk really brings back memories. It's the one I used when I worked with Flipper the seal.

[*He takes out some bells.*]

These are the bells he wore around his neck . . . tied with a big red bow.

[*He takes out a horn.*]

This horn brings back memories.

[*He blows it.*]

What an act! I used to blow the horn while Flipper would dance.

[*He takes out big ball.*]

Oh, what a finish this act had! There was Flipper walking across the stage on a wire, spinning a hoop around his neck, bouncing the ball on his nose, while I stood in a baby spot singing, "Always Think of Mother". . . This act laid off for about two years.

224

[*Dissolve to: Bedroom. Clothes are out. Grips, drawers open. General disarray.* Gracie *is trying to tidy up.* Von Zell *comes in.*]

Von Zell:

Gracie, I got your phone call and I rushed right over. What's all this? Are you moving?

Gracie:

No, George lost five dollars, and he's turned the whole house upside down looking for it. You should see the den.

Von Zell:

That doesn't sound like George.

Gracie:

That's why I called you over. I'm worried. I think it's affecting his mind, and he keeps muttering about baby pictures.

Von Zell:

Maybe that's what he's looking for.

Gracie:

Oh, no, I've seen those pictures. Harry, I love George, but when he was a baby, his face had no expression at all. In fact, the only picture with any personality was taken when he was lying on his stomach.

Von Zell:

I can't get over this. It can't be the five dollars. He's

working too hard. What George should do is lay off television a couple of months and take a rest. And you can tell him he doesn't have to worry about me. He's paid me well all these years. And I've got enough money to last me until tonight.

Gracie:
Thanks, he's lucky to have a friend like you.

Von Zell:
Yeah . . . wait a minute . . . George lost five dollars. All we have to do is pretend we found the five dollars and give it to him and the problem is over.

Gracie:
When I was at the Mortons', they said the same thing.

Von Zell:
I'm going down to talk to him.

Gracie:
That's a wonderful idea. I'll be down in a minute.

[Von Zell *starts out.*]

[*Cut to: Burns living room. Trunks are all around the room.* Von Zell *comes down the stairs. Reacts when he sees them.*]

Von Zell:
[*To himself*] Dragging up all these old trunks and looking through them for a five-dollar bill. Gee, he

must have really blown his top. I'd better humor him.

[George *comes in pushing a trunk.*]

George:
Hi, Harry, give me a hand with this trunk.

Von Zell:
Sure, George, I don't want you to hurt yourself.

[Von Zell *pretends to find a bill.*]

Hey, look what I just found on the floor! A five-dollar bill.

George:
Hey, that's mine. I lost it. Thanks.

[George *takes it.*]

Von Zell:
Now can I help you take the trunks back to the basement?

George:
No, I haven't looked through all of them yet.

[Von Zell *reacts.* Gracie *comes down the stairs.*]

Gracie:
George, you can stop worrying. I was up in the bedroom and I found your five dollars.

[Gracie *gives a bill to* George *and gives a big wink to* Von Zell.]

George:

[*Dubious*] Thanks.

> [George *looks at* Von Zell.]

Von Zell:

Er—Gracie, I want to talk to you.

> [Von Zell *takes* Gracie *aside*. Blanche *comes in from kitchen*.]

Blanche:

George, you can stop worrying. I found your five dollars in the kitchen.

> [Blanche *hands him a bill. Gives* Gracie *and* Von Zell *a wink*.]

George:

Thanks, Blanche.

Von Zell:

Blanche, we'd like to talk to you.

> [Blanche *moves over to them.* Harry *comes in French doors*.]

Harry:

George. . . .

> [George *puts his hand out*.]

George:

Where did you find it?

Harry:

On the patio.

Von Zell:

Harry. . . . Come with us. There's something we've got to discuss.

> [*The four move out onto the patio, closing the French doors.* George *looks in the camera.*]

George:

You see how careless I am. And I thought I only lost one five-dollar bill.

> [*Cut to: Burns patio.* Gracie, Blanche, Von Zell, *and* Harry.]

Von Zell:

How do you like that? He took five dollars from each of us.

Harry:

I must say that his phobia has certain financial advantages.

Blanche:

It's even worse than I thought. [*Points*] He's still looking in the trunks for the money.

Von Zell:

We can't handle this. George needs somebody who understands these cases and I know just the man . . . Dr. Bellamy. He has hundreds of nervous patients.

Blanche:

Good! Let's send for him.

I Love Her, That's Why!

Gracie:

I'm not so sure. He can't be so good if he makes all his patients nervous.

Von Zell:

Believe me, Gracie, he's great and I'm going to call him right now.

> [*They all start for the Morton house.*]
>
> [*Dissolve to: Morton living room. Harry, Von Zell and* Dr. Bellamy *are seated. They are having coffee. The* Doctor *is smoking a cigar.*]

Harry:

Have we given you a clear picture of the Burns case, Dr. Bellamy?

Bellamy:

Yes, an obvious example of the money neurosis.

Von Zell:

Well, what do you advise, Doc?

Bellamy:

Harry, I'd rather speak directly to Mrs. Burns. Is she here?

Harry:

Yes, she's in the kitchen with my wife, but it might be inadvisable for you to see her. She's . . . well, she's a bit peculiar.

Bellamy:

I thought it was the husband.

230

Von Zell:

Doc, Gracie is peculiar in a different way. If you tried to explain things to her you'd only get confused.

Bellamy:

Nonsense! I'm sure I can make myself understood. This is my business and I'm quite capable of handling it. Please, call her, Mr. Morton.

Harry:

[*Shrugs*] As you wish. [*Calls*] Blanche, will you and Gracie come in?

Bellamy:

I've never failed to get through to people, because I know how to reason with them.

[Blanche *and* Gracie *come in.*]

Harry:

Dr. Bellamy, this is my wife and this is Mrs. Burns.

[*They acknowledge.*]

Bellamy:

Please sit down, Mrs. Burns . . . here by me.

[Gracie *sits down.*]

These gentlemen have told me about your husband, and I'm sure the problem of the five dollars would leave his mind if he had something more important to worry about. Do you understand that?

Gracie:

Of course. You mean a bigger worry would make him forget the little worry.

231

I Love Her, That's Why!

Bellamy:

[*Beams at her*] Exactly.

[*He gives* Harry *and* Von Zell *a triumphant look.*]

This method seldom fails. As an example, I once had a patient who was losing his hair and thought he'd soon have none left on his head. It was a small thing but it worried him.

Gracie:

Oh, how ridiculous!

Bellamy:

Of course.

Gracie:

Why should he worry about that? Plenty of men have small heads.

[Doctor *reacts.*]

Von Zell:

Gracie, he meant that the man . . .

Bellamy:

I'll explain it, Harry. The man's head was of normal size, Mrs. Burns. He was just worried about losing his hair. The fear of getting bald caused him to become more and more nervous. This made his wife nervous, too.

Gracie:

Oh, they were both getting bald.

232

Bellamy:

No, no, just the husband. Soon he couldn't sleep or eat. All he did was rub hair tonic into his scalp.

Gracie:

Really?

Bellamy:

Yes, his wife tried to take his mind off it. She cooked him fried chicken, lobster . . . but he wouldn't touch them.

Gracie:

Well, I don't blame him. I wouldn't rub fried chicken or lobster into my scalp either.

Blanche:

Honey, he didn't rub the—

Bellamy:

[*To Blanche*] If you don't mind. [*To Gracie*] I mean he wouldn't eat them. He became worse and worse and his wife finally decided that he needed a shock to bring him to his senses.

Gracie:

What did she do?

Bellamy:

She consulted her lawyer. Then the lawyer went to her husband and said that she was planning to divorce him.

233

I Love Her, That's Why!

Gracie:

Oh, that must have been a shock!

Bellamy:

Yes, it was.

Gracie:

He probably didn't know that his wife was married to the lawyer.

Bellamy:

I didn't say that! She sent the lawyer to say that she was divorcing her husband. She wasn't married to him.

Gracie:

If she wasn't married to him how could she divorce him?

Bellamy:

They were married!

Gracie:

Who was?

Bellamy:

The lawyer and the wife . . . I mean the husband and the lawyer . . . I mean the wife and the husband!

[*As he says this he takes his cigar and stirs coffee with it. Camera does not show it.*]

Von Zell:

Doc, I told you you were going to get confused.

234

Bellamy:

I'm not confused!

Von Zell:

[*Points*] Then if I were you I'd use a spoon.

> [Bellamy *sees it. He puts cigar in ash tray.*]

Bellamy:

[*To Gracie*] Anyhow, the shock cured the woman's husband and she sent the lawyer away. Now he's completely bald but they're very happy together.

Gracie:

How do you like that? As soon as her husband's cured she starts running around with that bald-headed lawyer.

Bellamy:

[*Dazed*] Well, I did my best. Good-by.

> [*All say good-by. His hat and small black bag are on a table. He starts out.*]

Von Zell:

Doc, you forgot your hat.

Bellamy:

Oh, yes.

> [*He comes back. Picks up hat and starts out.*]

Von Zell:

And your satchel.

Bellamy:

Oh, yes.

[*He comes back, starts to pick up* Gracie.]

Gracie:

Good-by, everybody.

[Von Zell *stops* Bellamy *and gives him his bag and aims him for the door.*]

[*Cut to: Morton front door. Door is ajar and* George *is standing there. Doctor goes out. Off we hear* Blanche, Harry *and* Von Zell *laughing.*]

George:

Good-by, Dr. Bellamy.

Bellamy:

Good-by.

[*Still dazed,* Bellamy *leaves.*]

Von Zell:

[*Off*] I knew this would happen.

Harry:

[*Off*] But it was good advice.

Von Zell:

[*Off*] Look, Gracie, what my friend **Dr.** Bellamy was trying to tell you is, give George some bigger problem to worry about and he'll forget about the five dollars he lost.

Blanche:

[*Off*] And we'll drop in and see if it helped him.

> [George *reacts a bit, and quietly closes the door. Turns to camera.*]

George:

I hope this big problem doesn't take too long or Arthur Godfrey will have to solve it.

> [*Dissolve to: Burns living room. The trunks are gone.* George *is sitting there.* Gracie *comes in.*]

Gracie:

George. . . . I don't want to bother you at a time like this, but will you do me a favor?

George:

All right.

Gracie:

You know the two steaks I ordered at the market for dinner?

George:

Yes.

Gracie:

Well, call them and tell them to only send one. I'm divorcing you. [*Pause*] I guess our divorce is such a shock to you, you don't know what to say . . . huh?

George:

That's right. What is there to say?

I Love Her, That's Why!

Gracie:

Well . . . er . . . why don't you ask me why I'm divorcing you?

George:

I'm too shocked.

Gracie:

[*Brightens*] You are?

George:

But not enough to stop looking for the five dollars.

Gracie:

But, George. . . . If we get divorced it can ruin our happiness.

George:

It can even ruin our marriage.

Gracie:

Yes, that, too.

George:

Are your plans all set? Are you going to Reno?

Gracie:

No, first I think I'll get the divorce . . . then I might go to Reno.

George:

Good idea. Have you picked out a lawyer yet?

Gracie:

No, but I know the kind I want. He should be bald-

238

headed so he won't have to rub fried chicken in his hair.

George:

Yeah, that's the best kind. . . . When did you decide on that?

Blanche:

[*Off*] [*Calls*] Yoohoo . . . where is everybody?

Gracie:

[*To Herself*] Thank heavens! [*Calls*] In here, Blanche!

[Blanche, Harry *and* Von Zell *enter.*]

George, you talk to the boys. Come on, Blanche, help me fix some coffee.

Blanche:

Coffee?

[Gracie *winks at her, nudges her.*]

Gracie:

[*Sotto*] It's not working. Come on, Blanche.

[Gracie *goes off.* Blanche *starts to follow her.*]

George:

I'm glad you're all here. I've just had some shocking news. . . .

[Blanche *stops . . . to listen.*]

Von Zell:

Oh . . . no! George, I simply can't believe it.

239

I Love Her, That's Why!

George:

Wait . . . I haven't told you what it is.

> [Blanche *and* Harry *turn on* Von Zell.]

Blanche:

Yes, Von Zell . . . what's the matter with you?

Von Zell:

Yeah . . . well . . . no . . . I mean . . . any bad news upsets me.

George:

Well, anyway. . . . Gracie's divorcing me.

> [*They're all horrified. Ad lib exclamations like, What? . . . Oh, not really! etc.* George *looks at them.*]

What's the matter? Did you expect it to be more shocking?

Harry:

No . . . certainly not.

Von Zell:

We didn't expect it to be that bad.

Blanche:

What caused it?

> [Gracie *enters.*]

George:

Blanche, it's too late to pretend. Gracie is divorcing me. So she must have found out about us.

240

Blanche:

About *us?*

George:

Yes, our romance.

[Gracie *listens*. Harry *and* Von Zell *react.*]

Harry:

[*To Von Zell*] I didn't think he was *that* crazy.

George:

I knew this would catch up with us sooner or later. Blanche, we've been fools. We should have stopped this mad thing years ago.

Gracie:

George, how could you do this? And you, Blanche . . . you've been my best friend for years.

Blanche:

Gracie, he's only joking.

Gracie:

It might be a joke to him . . . but not for you. You must be desperate! With all the men in the world, you wind up with George and Harry.

[*Sound: Door chimes (Off)*.]

George:

[*Calls*] Come in. . . . Gracie, I was outside the Mortons' door and I heard the whole little plot you all cooked up.

I Love Her, That's Why!

[Ned Brown *enters.*]

Ned:

Hello, George. . . .

George:

Oh, Ned . . . You know Gracie . . . and Harry Von Zell. . . .

Ned:

Sure. Hello, Gracie . . .

Gracie:

And this is Blanche, George's sweetheart, and her husband, Harry.

Ned:

What?

George:

Just a little private joke. These are our next-door neighbors.

Ned:

Oh. George, I got your call and I'm so glad you found those baby pictures.

George:

I looked through every drawer, closet, and trunk in the house . . . but I finally found them. Here they are.

[George *takes them from a table. Hands them to* Ned. *The rest react.*]

242

Harry:

[*To Von Zell*] So that's what he was looking for.

Ned:

These'll be fine, George. Well, I'd better be going. Nice to have seen you all. . . . Oh, I almost forgot. Here's the five dollars you loaned me this morning for cab fare, George.

> [Ned *takes a bill out and gives it to* George.]

George:

So *that's* where that five-dollar bill went.

Ned:

Good-by, everybody.

> [*They all say good-by.* Ned *leaves.*]

George:

When are you people going to learn to mind your own . . .

Blanche:

George, as long as you're well again, we'd like our money back.

> [George *takes out the four fives. He passes out the bills.* Gracie *runs around, gets the fifth five.* George *looks at her.*]

George:

Well, I'm short a five again. That's where I came in.

> [*Music*]
>
> [*Applause*]

I Love Her, That's Why!

Well, that's our script and we do one every week. As I say, writing is a murderous job, because you're never away from it. You don't just put down the piece of paper and walk out of the studio—you take the plot and the jokes with you and work on them at dinner, in bed, and in the shower. It is endless, fatiguing, and frustrating work, and I don't understand why anybody would do it voluntarily. That's why it handed me a laugh when I got this letter from my publishers saying I should write a book. Write a *book!* And they finished their letter with this killer: "You undoubtedly work fast, so you could knock it out in six or seven months." I sat down and wrote them a letter:

GENTLEMEN:

I am pleased and flattered that you think the public would be interested in a book about me. However there are a few facts which you probably don't know. Gentlemen, I am a busy man. For your information, here is my week:

Monday I get up at seven and meet with my writers at eight. We work until we have a story line for that week's show—we're always three weeks ahead in our preparation. Sometimes we can develop a story in about seven hours, sometimes it's a full day's work. Tuesday I'm at the studio at nine-thirty to meet the cast and stage the show we are shooting that week— we do them on film, you know. Wednesday I get up at six and we shoot the show—we usually finish by seven at night. Thursday I meet my writers again. They bring in the stuff they've been working on that we lined up Monday. We break at twelve for lunch. On purpose we go to a terrible coffee shop we can't wait

244

to get out of so we'll be back in the office by twelve-thirty. We work until four. Friday the same writers and I meet at nine, and work again until four, in a closed room with no interruptions, including phone calls. Saturday morning I put together all the material we've been working on all week.

Saturday afternoon I get away from it all. I go to the Hillcrest Country Club where I sit at the round table with a lot of actors, directors, and producers—all with problems, and all talking about them and offering each other advice. Here I'm really busy. You know how it is, you never work so hard as when you're not being paid for it. Saturday night when I get home I'm greeted by the mimeographed script we finished that morning—this runs fifty-two pages and I have to cut it to forty-three while I'm dressing to take Gracie to a party.

Now, I am considered very good at sociables, so Saturday night I really kill myself. You see, Gracie's heard all my jokes and so has Jack Benny, so I have to work up some new endings to the old jokes before I get to the party. Sunday at nine, one of my secretaries arrives and I pre-cut the following week's shooting script. At ten, Freddy de Cordova, our producer-director, comes to the house to discuss the work completed since our last meeting, and we make final decisions about shooting procedures. Sunday night I look at TV to see what the other people are doing.

Oh, yes, I forgot to mention that I also have to memorize the show. I also forgot to mention that I'm president of McCadden Productions. McCadden films our own show, "The Bob Cummings Show," "Life with Father," and a lot of pilot films for CBS, as well as outside commercials. We also film "The People's Choice," which Irving Brecher produces and directs, starring Jackie Cooper, and a new dramatic series called "Impact" for NBC. Now on top of all this you want me to write a book, and "it will take *only* six or seven months"! As I say, this line really handed me a laugh. Gentlemen, I'll do it.

> Cordially,
> GEORGE BURNS, singer, dancer,
> roller skater, straight man,
> actor, writer, director,
> producer—author.

22

LAST January 23 the Friars Club held a Friars Frolic at the Biltmore Hotel in Los Angeles "to commemorate Burns and Allen's twenty-five years in show business." (It was really thirty years—I told the Friars twenty-five. I don't know—guess I just can't help it.) It was one of the nicest things that ever happened to us. The nicest part of the niceness was that they raised over a hundred thousand dollars for local charities. On the dais at the dinner was a gathering of people I wouldn't be a bit surprised if you've heard of before. There were Jack Benny; Danny Kaye; Doré Schary, head of MGM Studio; William Paley, head of the Columbia Broadcasting System; Samuel Goldwyn, head of Goldwyn Studios; George Jessel; Ronald Reagan; Eddie Cantor; Jimmy Cagney; Danny Thomas; William Goetz of Goetz Productions; and Tony Martin.

In the speeches some nice things were said about us. I can't repeat them, because it would sound immodest. Some of them I can't repeat for other rea-

247

sons. Danny Kaye said Gracie was "one of the kindest, loveliest, most illuminated women" he had ever
known. He said I was——. That's one of the ones I
can't tell you for the other reason. Doré Schary said,
"The first time I met George Burns, I had just become head of R.K.O. Pictures. I was pretty pleased
with myself. We were at a party and people were
settling down to playing cards. I drew Burns as a
partner, and as we started to play he rapped my
knuckles and said, 'Let me tell you something. I
want very much to get back into pictures, but make
one mistake and I'll spit in your eye.' "

All through the evening, there were lots of nice
things said about me that I really can't repeat.
Jessel said, "——— — —— ——" Cantor said, "—
— — —— — —— —— ——— ——— ———

———— ———" and the fellow that really surprised
me was Benny. He said, "— — — — — — — — —
— — — — — — — — — — — — — — — —
— — — — — — — — — — — — — — — —
— — — — — — — — — — — — — — — —
— — — — — — — — — — — —"

I sat there and blushed like a kid.

As I say, lots of nice things were said and lots of
nice things were done, such as Jimmy Cagney coming to the party despite the fact that he had a tem-
perature of 102 and was supposed to be in bed.

Gracie was terribly nervous for days before the
event, because her training was to talk to another
player onstage rather than directly to the audience.
The more nervous she got, the more nervous I got
for her—and I'm used to talking to audiences. The

248

upshot of it was, *she* spoke, was letter perfect, and *I* blew every line.

Later, on the way home, I said, "What happened? You were perfect—I thought you were nervous."

She said, "I was. But I was sitting near the speakers' rostrum and I noticed that everybody who got up to speak was nervous, and when I saw how nervous they were, I forgot to be." She also forgot to tell me she wasn't; so I was.

Everything about the evening made us happy, but I think the thing that made us happiest of all was the fact that out in front, applauding us harder than anybody, were our kids, Ronnie, Sandy, and her husband, Jim Wilhoite. The kids, although never interested in show business for themselves, always were for us, and have always been our biggest rooters. This night Gracie and I talked more about our children than anything else. There was such a feeling of the whole night being a milestone.

Twenty-five years (I mean thirty—there I go again) in a business, and having all your friends pat you on the back for your part in it, is a great sensation; but having your kids watch them do it is greater. But it was a little sad as well as joyful, because the kids were so grown up. Sandy looked beautiful, her figure all back from being a new mother. And Ronnie could have passed for a leading man. I'd like to say something about Jim Wilhoite, but let *his* father write a book.

Both our kids . . . something to be proud of, but both somehow slipping away from us. . . . Sandy is happy, and we see her and Jim and the baby all the time, but still. . . . What used to be her room is now a study; and when we walk by Ronnie's room with the walls covered with fishnets, boat lights, water skis and what not, aside from getting seasick we can't help but wonder how long it's going to look like that. It can't be long before he will go in the Army, or get married, or something.

Having Sandy go left a big hole in our house as well as our lives. When Ronnie goes too, it's going to be worse. He's a complete joy to have around, good-natured, no trouble, and a great audience for me—I absolutely kill him. He not only laughs at me, but cues me in. Sometimes when he has a group of friends in, I do as many as five shows a day. I'm going to miss that.

And it's going to be a terrible strain on Gracie. She already holds still for thirty-year-old jokes at parties; she should get a little rest around the house.

Ronnie hasn't yet decided what he wants to do, or be. Up to now, he's done everything for us, not for himself. He draws extremely well, so Gracie thought he might make a good architect. He worked at it, but it obviously wasn't for him. He knows I never quite gave up the hope that he might land in some form of show business, so he studied cinematography to please me. That wasn't it either. When he gets around to doing it for Ronnie, whatever it is, he'll be the best at it. It's his nature. Right now, he's probably the world's best baby sitter. And don't think Sandy doesn't utilize his talents. Every day, she has him over at her house watching the baby, or fixing things around the house.

250

The other day we had a big wind and a tree blew down in Sandy's yard. She was on the phone saying, "Send Ronnie over," five minutes after it happened. It doesn't occur to her that the same wind blew things down in our yard. It's getting so, if we need anything done I have to call Sandy's husband Jim away from the studio where he works, to come to our house and fix it, because Ronnie is at his house fixing something. Very confusing.

The love the children have always had for each other has been a wonderful thing to observe as they grew. They head the mutual-admiration society of all time. Oddly, the qualities they most admire in each other are the qualities they least admire in themselves. What Sandy considers her own weaknesses Ronnie considers her strengths, and vice versa. They are both having as much fun with Sandy and Jim's baby as if she were a new toy; as a matter of fact, I don't think Ronnie would even trade her for his surfboard.

And speaking of the baby, I'm going to be careful not to say anything that sounds like bragging, because there's nothing duller than a person who carries on about a grandchild. I'll only say, Laurie's the most beautiful, the brightest, makes the most amazing noises, and I'd be the last to claim a prodigy in the family but—would you believe it?—when you put out your finger she grabs it! And she can do it with either hand. Really!

This baby has been great for us, because it's like starting all over with Sandy and Ronnie. That's why, the other night after the Friars Frolic, when

I Love Her, That's Why!

Gracie and I were talking about what a milestone it was, and about the future, and our plans, that she laughed right in my face. I said, "Well, I guess we have to face the fact that Ronnie will go soon, and I suppose you and I will go back to where we started: a hotel. There's no point in our rattling around in this big house. We bought it for the children, and when they don't need it we should sell it."

That's when Gracie started to laugh. "Who doesn't need it?" she said. "I know you aren't very observant, but you should look around the house. The downstairs closet has a crib, car seat, blankets, box of diapers, and a carton of canned milk in it. The upstairs study has a play pen, high chair, and a swing in the middle of the floor . . . Laurie's not ready for them yet, but it won't be long. You can't mix a cocktail behind the bar because the bottle warmer is plugged in there. The library has—"

"I see what you mean," I said. "And I suppose by the time Laurie is too big for them, Ronnie will have one who can use them. I get the message—we keep the house."

Gracie is out now, Easter shopping for Laurie. This sort of a thing is very serious with her. Christmas, birthdays, Valentine's Day—anything, as long as she can give somebody a present. I never think of these things, because I know Gracie will. She's always had a fabulous enthusiasm for them. Like writing thank-you notes and that sort of thing, Gracie does them all by hand, herself. That's Gracie: if she does it, she goes all out. Not me; I'd do it differently—have my secretary type the letters. I'd have to. Jerry spells better than I do.

I always believe, "Lucky is the man who knows his limitations." I know mine. That's why I hire so many capable people who can do the job I'm not capable of doing. It generally takes four or five people to replace one person's weakness in an organization. I've got about seventy-five working for me. However, I'm apparently not the only one aware of my limitations.

The other day I was walking on Beverly Drive and I couldn't believe my eyes. I saw Miss Klein, my old teacher from P.S. 22. I ran toward her, but not very fast. I said, "I beg your pardon—aren't you Miss Klein?"

She said, "Yes."

I said, "You probably don't remember me, but I was a student of yours. Nathan Birnbaum. I sang with the Pee Wee Quartette."

"How could I forget you?—you were in my class for four years," she said.

I said, "Miss Klein, this may come as a shock to you but I have just written a book."

She said, "Birnbaum, you never were bright, but at least as a child you never were a liar."

I took her address, and I shall send Miss Klein a book. I shall give one to Gracie, and I may or may not give one to Mary Livingston's husband. This depends upon the way the prologue is handled.

Speaking of Jack writing the prologue to the book, I know what he's going to say. He's going to say he hasn't read the book. This is not true. Not that Jack would lie intentionally, but I know he'll lock the door, read the book, and *then* write the prologue. Jack, this is personal to you: Read this paragraph

253

carefully: Say what you want about me. If you think I'm nice, say I'm nice. If you think I'm mean, say I'm mean. I want this book completely honest. But before you start to write, I want to tell the readers something: I think Jack Benny is the kindest, finest, nicest, handsomest, biggest, most talented and the most generous man I ever knew. . . . Now, Jack, write the prologue!

Hey, what goes? I'm on page 254—it's time to wrap this up. You know, it's a murderous job, ending a book. I've been trying for about twenty pages. I just can't get off. But I want something different. I want a great ending that has class, dignity, something people will remember. You know, like Tolstoy's *War and Peace*—now that's a great finish. Why not? If it's good enough for Tolstoy, it's certainly good enough for me.

". . . But just as in astronomy, the new view said, 'It is true, we do not feel the movement of the earth, but, if we admit its immobility, we are reduced to absurdity, while admitting its movement, we are led to laws'; so in history, the new view says, 'It is true, we do not feel our dependence, but admitting our free will, we are led to absurdity; admitting our dependence on the external world, time, and cause, we are led to laws.'

"In the first case, we had to surmount the sensation of an unreal immobility in space, and to admit a motion we could not perceive of by sense. In the present case, it is as essential to surmount a consciousness of an unreal freedom and to recognize a dependence not perceived by our senses."

The End

254

TEAR
HERE

DEAR READER:
I just read George's book and I enjoyed it very much.

But there's one little thing I'd like to straighten out. However, if George finds out I told you, he wouldn't be fit to live with. He never did pay back that four hundred dollars.

Now please tear this page out.

Love,
GRACIE

TEAR
HERE

Index

Levee, Mike, 194
Leviathan, 129, 131
Levy, Ralph, 195
"Life of Peter Stuyvesant, The," 20
"Life with Father," 245
Linder, Jack, 45
Linelli, Louis, 28, 29
Little Puss, 23
Livingston, Mary (Mrs. Jack Benny), 89, 124, 161, 253
Loew's circuit, 69, 103, 104, 107
Loew's Roof, New York, 58
Loew's Theater, 86th Street, New York, 103, 104
Loew's Theater, Providence, 66
Lombardo, Guy, 148, 149, 157
Lombardy, The, New York, 163
London, England, 129
London, Tower of, 134
Lorraine, Billy, 74–77, 79, 81, 82
Los Angeles, California, 77, 175
Louie, 12
Ludwig, Dr., 181

Lyons, Arthur, 143, 144, 167

M

Malone, Janie, 55
Mangin Street, New York, 7, 8
"Many Happy Returns," 157
Maple Drive, Beverly Hills, 167
Marcus, Farley, 57, 90, 91
Martin, Tony, 247
Marx, Groucho, 188
Marx, Harpo, 188
Marx, Mike, 65, 73
"Mary Ann, Mary Ann, Mary Sat in a Corner," 23
Mayfair (Columbia) Theater, 93
M.C.A., *see* Music Corporation of America
McCadden Productions, 245
McCann, Walter, 70, 71
McGiviney, Owen, 160
Mechanicsville, New York, 35
Medbury, John P., 137, 189, 190
"Melancholy Baby," 188
Menominee, Michigan, 177
Michaels, Joe, 89, 90

Pee Wee Presbyterian
  Quartette, 28
Pee Wee Quartette, 5–6,
  10, 13, 17, 19, 20, 23, 24,
  27, 29, 47, 253
"People's Choice, The,"
  245
Philadelphia, Pennsylva-
  nia, 78
Pinaud, Ed, and Company,
  37
Pinfeather, Chief, 177
Pissano, General, 99–100
Pitkin Avenue, Browns-
  ville, 23, 53
Pitt Street, New York, 3
Pittsburgh, Pennsylvania,
  74
Portland, 76, 112
Proctor's Theater, Mount
  Vernon, 126
Proctor's Theater, New-
  awk, 75
P.S. 22, 7, 8, 16, 253
P.S. 188, 58
Putnam Building, New
  York, 45

R

"Ragging the Scale," 47
Reagan, Ronald, 247
Reber, John, 148
Red, 182
Red Bank, New Jersey, 55

Red Cross, 174
Red Leaf Circle Club, New
  York, 39
Red Ribbons, 11, 12
"Red Rose Rag, The," 49
Reilly, Larry, 102, 163
Reilly, Larry, and Com-
  pany, 86
"Religion Versus Love," 14
Riverside Theater, New
  York, 162
Rivington Street, New
  York, 4, 27
R.K.O. Pictures, 248
Robert Burns Panatellas,
  148
Rockford, Micky, 194
"Roll Those Bones," 23
Romanoff's, 194, 195
Ronkonkoma, 57
Roosevelt, Eleanor, 179
Rose (nurse), 168
Rose and Curtis, 75
Rosebud Sisters, 62, 65, 66
Rosenzweig's candy store,
  6–7, 21, 24
Roth, Murry, 143
Runyon, Damon, 187

S

St. Malachy's Church, 122
San Francisco, California,
  76, 77, 86, 112
Santa Claus, 190

Index

About the Authors

GEORGE BURNS: You can read all about him in the book.

CYNTHIA HOBART LINDSAY: Having been educated in an expensive girls' finishing school, Cynthia Hobart Lindsay promptly became a stunt woman— falling off horses and cliffs, swimming in aquacades, skating and skiing in Sonja Henie movies, and riding covered wagons across the plains. When she gave up stunting she began to write, first for M-G-M and later as a free-lancer for magazines. She is still writing for magazines and she still lives in California, with her husband Louis Lindsay, her children Meg and Michael, and her poodles Beetle and Doc.

CPSIA information can be obtained at www.ICGtesting.com
Printed in the USA
LVOW072124160212

268940LV00004B/395/P